Gangs

Other titles in the Hot Topics series include:

Gangs

by Jenny MacKay

LUCENT BOOKS
A part of Gale, Cengage Learning

Detroit • New York • San Francisco • New Haven, Conn • Waterville, Maine • London

LIBRARY OF CONGRESS CATALOGING-IN-PUBLICATION DATA

MacKay, Jenny, 1978–
  Gangs / by Jenny MacKay.
    p. cm. -- (Hot topics)
  Includes bibliographical references and index.
  ISBN 978-1-4205-0343-2 (hbk.)
  1. Gangs--United States--Juvenile literature. I. Title.
  HV6439.U5M25 2010
  364.1'0660973--dc22

                                        2010027974

Lucent Books
27500 Drake Rd.
Farmington Hills, MI 48331

ISBN-13: 978-1-4205-0343-2
ISBN-10: 1-4205-0343-X

Printed in the United States of America
1 2 3 4 5 6 7 14 13 12 11 10

Printed by Bang Printing, Brainerd, MN, 1st Ptg., 10/2010

CONTENTS

FOREWORD

Young people today are bombarded with information. Aside from traditional sources such as newspapers, television, and the radio, they are inundated with a nearly continuous stream of data from electronic media. They send and receive e-mails and instant messages, read and write online "blogs," participate in chat rooms and forums, and surf the Web for hours. This trend is likely to continue. As Patricia Senn Breivik, the former dean of university libraries at Wayne State University in Detroit, has stated, "Information overload will only increase in the future. By 2020, for example, the available body of information is expected to double every 73 days! How will these students find the information they need in this coming tidal wave of information?"

Ironically, this overabundance of information can actually impede efforts to understand complex issues. Whether the topic is abortion, the death penalty, gay rights, or obesity, the deluge of fact and opinion that floods the print and electronic media is overwhelming. The news media report the results of polls and studies that contradict one another. Cable news shows, talk radio programs, and newspaper editorials promote narrow viewpoints and omit facts that challenge their own political biases. The World Wide Web is an electronic minefield where legitimate scholars compete with the postings of ordinary citizens who may or may not be well-informed or capable of reasoned argument. At times, strongly worded testimonials and opinion pieces both in print and electronic media are presented as factual accounts.

Conflicting quotes and statistics can confuse even the most diligent researchers. A good example of this is the question of whether or not the death penalty deters crime. For instance, one study found that murders decreased by nearly one-third when the death penalty was reinstated in New York in 1995. Death penalty supporters cite this finding to support their argument that the existence of the death penalty deters criminals from committing murder. However, another study found that states without the death penalty have murder rates below the national average. This study is cited by opponents of capital punishment, who reject the claim that the death penalty deters murder. Students need context and clear, informed discussion if they are to think critically and make informed decisions.

The Hot Topics series is designed to help young people wade through the glut of fact, opinion, and rhetoric so that they can think critically about controversial issues. Only by reading and thinking critically will they be able to formulate a viewpoint that is not simply the parroted views of others. Each volume of the series focuses on one of today's most pressing social issues and provides a balanced overview of the topic. Carefully crafted narrative, fully documented primary and secondary source quotes, informative sidebars, and study questions all provide excellent starting points for research and discussion. Full-color photographs and charts enhance all volumes in the series. With its many useful features, the Hot Topics series is a valuable resource for young people struggling to understand the pressing issues of the modern era.

INTRODUCTION

GANGS ACROSS AMERICA

They number in the thousands. All together, they are 1 million members strong. No major city in America is without them, and they are in thousands of towns, suburbs, and even rural areas across the country. They are not limited to any one culture, ethnicity, gender, or age. They live mostly outside of the law, and their brutal, violent behavior knows few bounds. They are responsible for as much as 80 percent of the crime that occurs in the communities they call home. They are the gangs of America.

Gangs create legal and social issues all across the United States. Virtually all of the nation's cities are riddled with stories of widespread lawlessness and violence related to groups of people who have shunned school and legitimate jobs to live a life of crime. Gangs are often presented by the media as a contemporary problem; however, they have been a constant feature of America throughout most of its history. Their populations have surged during periods of immigration in almost every generation, especially in poor neighborhoods of big cities where immigrants have tended to cluster together for support and security in a new land that seems to offer them few chances to prosper. From the Italian, Jewish, and Irish gangs that ruled underclass neighborhoods of cities like Chicago and New York in the late 1800s to the criminal gangs of immigrants from Asia and Central and South America that exist in the nation's big cities today, immigrant gangs have made significant and often violent contributions to crime throughout American history. However, gangs are not created out of the stresses of immigration alone, nor are immigrant groups the only population from which gangs draw their members. Gangs form among every ethnic group, including whites and African Americans.

Sociologists, law enforcement agencies, youth specialists, and others who study gangs have learned that gangs seem to arise wherever and whenever people feel left out of mainstream society and have lost a sense of hope for the future. Gangs form among kids and teenagers, men and women, felons who are in prison, and veterans of war. Some gangs come and go quickly. Others survive for multiple generations. But the gang phenomenon itself is a long-standing feature of most American cities—and now of suburbs and towns as well. Researchers say gangs are growing, both in number and size.

This nineteenth-century print depicts the overcrowded conditions in New York City's Five Points district in the 1840s.

Statistics about gang crime, violence, and their ever-expanding size and numbers are important issues for community leaders, police departments, and citizens concerned about the safety and well-being of their gang-infested cities and towns. But statistics alone cannot give an accurate picture of gangs. Many who live near them, study them, or belong to one often find different truths about gangs than what statistics may lead the general public to believe. Although most gangs operate as criminal enterprises with a long track record of drug use and reckless violence, many of the people who belong to them also consider gangs to be caring families, reliable employers, and loyal protectors. And although gangs have become a common and negative topic in the media in recent decades, gangs also enjoy great popularity in media-generated pop culture. The public is fascinated by gang-related media and has given top box-office honors to many gang movies, while gang-related rap music frequently tops the charts. Although gangs are often violent, mysterious, and poorly understood by mainstream society, American culture nonetheless glorifies them and often portrays them as heroic enterprises.

Despite their sometimes glorified image, gangs can have very serious consequences for society. The gang culture is primarily one of crime, drug abuse, deadly violence, poverty, run-down neighborhoods, and the destruction of gang members' futures, since many gangsters are either killed on the streets by rival gangs or sent to prison for committing gang-related crimes. Knowing why and how gangs form, what triggers their violent or criminal ways, and why new members join them despite the risks to their personal safety and freedom could help researchers and communities address gang-related problems. Police forces and civic leaders in communities across America are coming together to search for ways to reduce gang violence and crime and deter people from joining gangs.

Although myths and mysteries have surrounded American gangs for hundreds of years, gang violence and crime are very real, and so are the socioeconomic factors that most experts believe give rise to gangs in so many different communities across the country. To their members, gangs are important social institutions. The rest of society cannot treat them merely as things to be feared, dreaded, and removed from the world. Instead, it must work to separate fiction about gangs from the realities of gang life. Understanding the gang phenomenon is a crucial step in responding to what many see as the growing crisis of American gangs. They are an issue of concern as well as controversy across the United States.

CHAPTER 1

THE HISTORY OF GANGS IN AMERICA

Youth groups have banded together in the United States al-most since the arrival of the first European colonists in the 1600s. As victims of a harsh and uncertain life of poverty, dis-ease, and near starvation, the early colonists were forced to focus their limited resources on just surviving. This was especially dif-ficult for children and teenagers, many of whom became orphans when their parents died from starvation or disease. Left without families and in many cases without much help or guidance from adults, some young immigrants formed groups and faced do-or-die choices in order to survive from one day to the next. These early "youth gangs" became a form of surrogate family for each other, providing companionship and a sense of security, or strength in numbers. Their situation was vastly different from modern urban America, but some of the forces that drove these earliest youth gangs together are similar to the driving forces be-hind gang populations in nearly every major U.S. city today.

Poverty, fear, lack of a loving and structured family, and the absence of positive adult guidance have always been factors at the heart of American gangs. Combined with a feeling of dis-placement, either because of immigration or an environment of social inequality, these are ingredients for the formation of gangs. Gangs have existed throughout United States history, usually deep within cities but always on the outskirts of main-stream, or typical, society. Gangs have grown during certain pe-riods of history, while at other times their populations have waned. Gang participants have been different ages and ethnici-ties and spoken many different languages over the years. They have been blamed for many of society's problems; they have been touted, too, as products of those problems. Through it all, gangs have been a constant phenomenon in American history.

Gangs Defined

During the time of the American colonies, the bands of orphaned children staying together for companionship and survival lacked some of the features of what today is classified as a gang. According to the U.S. Department of Justice, "One common definition of a gang is a group of three or more individuals who engage in criminal activity and identify themselves with a common name or sign."[1] By this definition, criminal activity is a central part of the gang problem and separates true gangs from other groups with names, such as sports teams, clubs, or college

Gangs like the "Short Tail" gang terrorized New York City's east side with their criminal activities in the 1880s.

fraternities and sororities. If America's first gangs were orphaned children of colonists, any crimes they committed, such as theft of food, were likely motivated by sheer desperation. Far different were some of the gangs that sprouted later, once cities had developed in America. For these gangs, crime was not just a survival mechanism; for many, it became a pastime.

Criminal gangs first began to flourish in U.S. cities in the 1800s. It was a time of heavy immigration, when thousands of people from European countries came to America in search of a better way of life. Irish, Italian, and Jewish immigrants flocked to the United States, but instead of the American dream of wealth and equality that many were seeking, they instead found racism, poverty, and an inner-city environment that was overcrowded, hostile, and dangerous. They began to form gangs that fit the modern definition well: they had names, they had distinct territories within cities like New York, and violent crime became a lifestyle for them.

Gangs as a Response to Social Problems

To understand why gangs seemed to form so readily among immigrants in the 1800s, sociologists have examined the way they lived. Nineteenth-century gangs, in large part, seem to have been a widespread and natural human response to intolerable living conditions. Gangs developed among all the major groups of immigrants coming to the United States in the nineteenth century, but most famously among the Irish and Italians. These immigrants lived in extremely filthy, crowded places. Some slept ten to a room in inner-city slum dwellings that lacked running water and flushing toilets. Most immigrants were uneducated and not qualified for high-paying jobs. For Italians, finding work was even more difficult because many did not yet speak English. Most of the jobs immigrants could find involved long hours of hard work for very little pay, sometimes not even enough to buy housing and food.

Making matters worse, many Americans did not like the immigrant groups that were arriving in growing numbers in the 1800s. They developed demeaning ethnic names for immigrants—such as Paddies or Micks for the Irish and WOPs,

In the 1800s, Italian immigrants lived in slums, held menial jobs, and were disliked by Americans. In response they developed their own racist behaviors and formed gangs as a means of self-preservation.

meaning "without papers" or "working on pavement," for Italians—and they resisted allowing immigrants into the mainstream American neighborhoods, jobs, or lifestyle. Journalist and historian David Kale describes how Americans in Boston treated Irish immigrants in the early 1800s. They would "rampage through Irish neighborhoods, where they shouted racial slurs, beat up passersby, [and] smashed windows,"[2] he says. The Italians fared no better. They too lived in slums, were disliked by Americans, held mostly menial jobs such as trash collecting, and lived in fear of being evicted by cruel landlords if they could not pay their rent.

Perhaps in response to the violence and bullying they endured, newly formed immigrant gangs developed their own

The Wildest Gangs

In the late 1800s, the slums of American cities spawned many urban gangs, but at the same time, another kind of gang ran rampant in America's open countryside, a lawless region known as the Wild West. Unlike city gangs that occupied well-defined neighborhoods, gangs of the Wild West were mobile and claimed a vast territory in which to carry out their crimes. They stole cattle and horses, robbed banks, held up trains and stagecoaches, and shot anyone who got in their way. These gangs, ruled by such infamous outlaws as Billy the Kid, Butch Cassidy, Wild Bill Hickock, and Jesse James, terrorized law-abiding citizens throughout the latter half of the nineteenth century. Their nomadic nature made them a persistent threat—one never knew where they would strike next. It also made them hard to capture. The lives of many Wild West gangsters ended violently in gunfights with law enforcement officers or other gangs. By the early 1900s, with the advent of automobiles, highways, and growing towns and cities, the lawlessness of the West disappeared, and with it, the West's worst outlaws. But these pistol-toting bandits hold a respected place in the history of American gangsters.

The Wild Bunch gang led by Butch Cassidy, seated, right, and The Sundance Kid, seated, center, terrorized railroads and citizens in the late nineteenth century.

racist behaviors, not just against Americans but against other immigrant groups. "Gang battles were extremely brutal, and men were killed with knives, hatchets, cleavers, and anything else that could puncture or slice flesh,"[3] says criminology professor Larry J. Siegel. There was an especially strong rivalry between the Irish and Italians, and as the immigrant population in America swelled in the mid- to late 1800s, violence between immigrant groups became a fact of life in inner cities. "Some Italians carried weapons partly to protect themselves from attacks by men of other nationalities, particularly the Irish,"[4] says Thomas A. Reppetto, former president of the New York City Crime Commission.

A NATIONAL THREAT

"We have a fundamental obligation to protect our American citizens from the threat posed by gang violence."—Russ Bergeron, U.S. Immigration and Naturalization Service media director.

Quoted in Tim McGurk, "Gangs: The Mara Salvatrucha," *Time*, July 27, 2008.

Hostile surroundings and the need for self-protection drove immigrants in America's cities to unite within their own nationality and to hate and fear other ethnic groups. They lay claim to particular neighborhoods of their cities and were wary of any intruders or strangers. Many historians and sociologists say that the violent, territorial nature of immigrant groups was a response to the racism and impoverished conditions of the overcrowded cities they lived in. "Youth and other community violence are a function of civil unrest and upheaval," says humanities researcher Steven David Valdivia. "As social conditions worsen in an area, violence increases."[5]

Branching off into distinct territories within cities may have been a survival technique for ethnic groups who felt threatened and vulnerable, but it also created the perfect environment for criminal street gangs. As immigrants in cities such as New York and Chicago lay claim to particular neighborhoods, they also invented names for themselves and began turning to crime as a way to earn extra money and gain a sense of power in an American society that had shunned them. Adding to the problem was the orphaned nature of immigrants. Many were young men who had set out on their own to start a new life in America; others had come to America with their families but were left alone and unsupervised while their parents worked long hours at low-paying jobs to make ends meet. "Regardless of their motives," says Reppetto, "young men far from home were good candidates for trouble."[6]

At first, when these young men joined one another and formed some of the first American gangs, such as the mostly Irish Whyos gang in New York City in the late 1860s, they resorted to crimes like gambling and getting into fistfights with rival gangs. The gangs and their growing criminal ways were separate from and even ignored by the rest of American society.

This nineteenth-century print depicts gang activity in New York's Five Points district in 1827.

Gang territories, or turfs, were considered bad parts of town and were completely avoided by outsiders, even by law enforcement officers. "Criminals and gang members had little to fear from the police as long as they stuck to their own neighborhoods,"[7] says Reppetto. Eventually, however, the gang population grew so large and its criminal ways so powerful that gang crime began to spill over into surrounding communities. No longer seen as a mere product of the social problems of the times, gangs also became a significant *cause* of social strife and upheaval in America by the early 1900s.

Gangs as a Cause of Social Problems

Immigrants to America, although largely shunned by the rest of American society, soon became too large a population for mainstream Americans to simply ignore. By 1910, says Reppetto, the city of New York had become "a metropolis where nearly three-quarters of the inhabitants were either immigrants or children of immigrants."[8] Increasing numbers of these ethnic groups belonged to gangs, a phenomenon that had begun to thrive in slum neighborhoods—such as a block of Manhattan known as the Five Points and home to some of America's first organized criminal gangs. Irish gangs in the Five Points—such as the Dead Rabbits and the Pug Uglies, ran gambling and prostitution rings and brutally fought outsiders to protect their turf from other gangs. A powerful Jewish gang known as the Monk Eastmans vied for control of the area as well. Meanwhile, an Italian gang network was gaining strength in the Five Points by the early 1900s and became known as the American Mafia, or the Mob. Fistfights, knife fights, and shootouts between gangs plagued the streets of New York City. Nongang citizens demanded that something be done. Police attempted to crack down on the problem. But some powerful members of the mainstream culture began to see gangs as a potential advantage.

Politicians, particularly those in big cities like New York and Chicago, recognized that as gangs grew in size and power, they could coerce people to vote for one politician over another and even scare voters away from the polls to prevent them from casting ballots for certain candidates. The 1900s brought about the start of a political era in which politicians, police, and gang leaders began forming corrupt alliances. Some gangs had grown wealthy from crime and powerful because of their violent and fearsome ways. They paid off police to avoid arrest. They also were courted by politicians who used gangs' power to get elected. Once these politicians were in office, they returned the favor by protecting gangs from police investigation. Gangs grew in size, wealth, political connections, and influence until they ruled America's largest cities in the first few decades of the 1900s. Whereas before, American society tended to view gangs as unfortunate products of miserable living conditions, by the early 1900s, gangs were seen as agents of terror, crime, and corruption.

Gangs and Organized Crime

The foothold of gangs in American society reached a peak shortly after the end of World War I, when the Eighteenth Amendment to the Constitution was ratified in 1919. The amendment banned alcohol within U.S. borders and made it illegal to manufacture, drink, or import the substance. The policy was known as Prohibition. Many American citizens rebelled against the new policy and laws, and secretive saloons called speakeasies sprang up all over the country. Supplying illegal liquor to these establishments became the most profitable criminal enterprise of the 1920s. Gangs, already entrenched in city life and largely protected by corrupt police and politicians, stepped up to run the illegal alcohol trade. They employed people to smuggle booze into the secretive speakeasies, a crime that was called bootlegging because the criminals sometimes hid bottles of alcohol inside their boots. What came next was an era of gang-related crime, power, terror, and murder that rocked American society, particularly in the cities of Chicago and New York. These were the places where the deadliest and most notorious mobsters—among them Lucky Luciano, Dutch Schultz, Bugs Moran, and the infamous Al Capone—rose to power by achieving great wealth from the illegal alcohol trade. They used their money to bribe police officers and elected officials into ignoring their illegal activities. Anyone they could not bribe, they

A Violent Valentine's Day

On the evening of February 14, 1929, seven men affiliated with the liquor-smuggling gang of mobster Bugsy Moran met in a Chicago warehouse, thinking they were there to buy cheap booze. Bugsy arrived late. When he drove up, he saw a police car on the street and fled, assuming a police raid was in progress. Inside the warehouse, the seven men—five members of Bugsy's gang, plus an optometrist and a mechanic—were facing a wall, believing they were about to be arrested for trying to buy alcohol during Prohibition. Instead, four men in police uniforms pulled out machine guns and shot the captives in the back, killing all of them before leaving the scene.

An intense investigation into the shootings revealed that the four killers were hit men and had most likely been hired by Bugsy Moran's worst enemy, mobster Al Capone. Capone was in Florida at the time of the killings and was never tried for having anything to do with the crime. If Capone really meant to have Moran killed, the night was a failure. Nonetheless, the incident, which became known as the St. Valentine's Day Massacre, is among history's most memorable and horrifying examples of gang-related violence.

Four of gangster Bugs Moran's men lie dead in the Chicago Clark Street garage that was the scene of the St. Valentine's Day Massacre in 1929.

murdered. Gang leaders were wanton killers who ruled by terror, ordering the deaths of anyone who got in their way. They hired assassins, called hit men, who killed enemies by stabbing them, shooting them, strangling them, rigging their vehicles with bombs, throwing them out the windows of tall buildings, and other terrifying methods. The violent tactics of these Prohibition-era gangs earned them brutal reputations that have contributed to the negative public opinion of gangs ever since.

PREYING ON SOCIETY

"They're not unlike wolves. They travel in packs. They do their crimes in packs. They socialize in packs."—Tim Twining, chief deputy district attorney, Denver, Colorado.

Quoted in "Mile High Killers," *Gangland Season 4*, DVD, produced by Steven Feinartz and Tracy Ullman, A&E Home Video, 2009.

During the Prohibition era, many of society's worst ills—including street violence, prostitution, murders, bribery, and corrupt police departments and politicians—were blamed on gangs. Prohibition was repealed in 1933, and the U.S. government began a campaign to end political corruption, lock up gang bosses, and stamp out the menacing gang problem that for years had run wild in America. For a while, the crackdown on gangs seemed to work. By the early 1940s, when the United States was fighting in World War II, there was a period of relative peace, patriotism, and crimelessness within the nation. Gangs, for a while, seemed a thing of the past. But the gang trend had not been permanently broken.

"Gang behavior and gang development tend to run in 'cycles,'" says sociology professor Donald J. Shoemaker. "That is, gang membership seems to swing in cycles involving as much as five or ten years.... Efforts to curb, reduce, or prevent gang activity may reflect cyclical patterns of gang membership and behavioral patterns as much as the efforts of the gang prevention programs."[9] The government's crackdown on gangs had not entirely succeeded, and America's gang issues had not vanished. They had merely gone dormant. In the years following World War II, the gang cycle once again swelled inside America's cities, and although the new gangs were culturally different than the immigrant gangs that came before them, the same kinds of social forces drove them together.

Different Era, Similar Social Problems

By the 1950s and 1960s, American society had mostly come to terms with its Irish, Italian, and Jewish citizens, and European immigration had slowed considerably. But cultural differences among Americans were far from over. New immigrants from Central and South America and Asia arrived in the United States and found much of the same cultural intolerance, poor living conditions, and lack of good jobs that had beset the immigrants of a century before. In response to these conditions, Hispanic and Asian youths condensed in American cities in the mid-1900s and began to form new gangs. The Latin Kings, for example, a gang of Puerto Rican immigrants, formed in Chicago in the late 1950s. In the same decade, Mexican immigrants in Southern California formed a gang called Nuestra Familia (Our Family). Chinese immigrants, meanwhile, were banding together in cities like San Francisco, where they formed the Joe Boys gang and the Yu Li gang in the 1960s. These and other gangs of immigrants were ancestors to some of the gangs that still exist in America today. They also provided evidence that immigrating to America created social conditions ripe for the formation of gangs, regardless of the ethnicity of the immigrants.

It was not just immigrants who felt displaced in American society. Black Americans, too, faced poverty and slums, racism and inequality. The era of social activism against racial segregation during the 1960s, known as the civil rights movement, was a time of extreme social strife between black and white Americans. Many social and legal changes during this time brought blacks and whites closer to social equality than ever before in American history, but interracial violence and prejudice also made some blacks feel as if they were being shoved to the edges of society. Many black gangs formed in America's cities during the 1950s and 1960s, such as the Vice Lords in Chicago, the Crips and the Bloods in Los Angeles, and the Black Spades in the Bronx of New York City. "The gang offered what [African American teenagers] absolutely needed to survive—protection, food and shelter, a sense of belonging, and self-esteem,"[10] says David Fattah, cofounder of the Philadelphia-based gang prevention program House of UMOJA and a former gang member himself in the 1960s. Gangs that formed in the mid-1900s, both among immigrant groups and among African Americans, had numerous similarities to gangs of the 1800s. Some of the same gangs, and many newer groups like them, still exist on the streets of America today.

Gangs Across Races

The tendency of people to form gangs seems to be a natural human response to an environment of social struggles, regardless of their race or culture. Americans from any cultural group, when they feel shunned by greater society, have been known to band together into criminal gangs, as was the case for many veterans of the Vietnam War in the 1960s and 1970s. The Vietnam War engendered another period of intense social unrest in America. Many Americans were opposed to the war and protested against it and the soldiers who fought in it. Veterans who returned home from Vietnam often felt like outcasts, unwanted and disrespected by society. In the late 1970s, some Vietnam veterans purchased motorcycles and turned against mainstream America, vowing to live on the outskirts of society. They gave rise to multiple outlaw motorcycle gangs, including the Bandidos, the Pagans, the Outlaws, and the Hells Angels, all of which still exist today. Outlaw motorcycle gangs consist mainly of white men in their twenties, thirties, and forties and are a violent social problem in many American cities. Culturally different than the black, Hispanic, and Asian gangs that also contribute to the modern gang population of America, motorcycle gangs can nonetheless be traced back to the same kinds of social strife and feelings of being outcasts that have been at the heart of gang formation in America throughout time.

In the 1960s, many returning Vietnam War veterans formed outlaw biker gangs.

The Modern American Gang

Gangs today represent a continuous negative force in the United States. Most gangs are still a product of impoverished inner-city environments and the shunning of certain groups by mainstream society, factors that have contributed to gang formation for centuries. Modern gangs continue to be a widespread social phenomenon in American society, and they are constantly growing in size and number. Attempts to define them, classify them, and react to them have given researchers interesting snapshots of the culture of modern gangs. Understanding that culture may be the key to addressing the social problems that gangs cause as well as the social problems that seem to cause them.

GANGS AND CULTURE

Gangs may not be a new phenomenon, but they are a current concern in America's communities. The United States' National Gang Center conducts regular surveys of gang populations and demographics in the nation's communities. Its 2010 estimates indicated that about twenty thousand different gangs exist in America, and they total about 1 million members. Gangs are still, as they have been throughout history, most common in the country's bigger cities. Ninety-nine percent of police departments in cities with more than one hundred thousand people report the presence of gangs in their area. Yet only 56 percent of the country's gang members live in major cities like Los Angeles, Chicago, or New York. The other 44 percent reside in small cities that have fewer than one hundred thousand people, in suburban communities, and in rural areas outside of cities, which are the places where gang activity is growing the fastest. Gangs are not just a "city problem" anymore.

In an effort to find ways to prevent the spread of existing gangs and the formation of new ones, social scientists study gang populations, looking for trends in the way gangs form and the reasons why people join them. Throughout their long history, American gangs have seemed to follow similar patterns. In particular, they have been considered a stand-in for families when normal family ties fail, especially in the inner-city environment. Gangs also seem to separate from mainstream society along ethnic lines, as well as by age, gender, and economic standing. The cultural characteristics that most gangs seem to have in common could provide researchers with an understanding of how and why gangs form.

Gang members and researchers who study gangs say that gangs serve an important social purpose—they provide a sense of family, belonging, and cultural identity for members who have not found other ways to meet these basic human needs. Much gang research has shown gangs to be alike in certain ways, suggesting that all gangs may provide their members with similar benefits and that these are people's main reasons for joining. Other researchers warn against jumping to conclusions about gangs, however. Categorizing gangs by their cultural similarities may only stereotype the gang phenomenon. There *are* similarities in the culture of America's thousands of gangs, but whether these trends reflect actual causes for the formation of gangs or provide the key to reversing gang growth is far less certain.

The Ethnic Trend in Gangs

Throughout history, American gangs have formed along ethnic lines. Immigrant groups banded together in the 1800s and early 1900s, leading to gangs that were defined by ethnicity, such as Irish, Italian, and Jewish. These cultural groups, like immigrant groups today, were drawn together in part by a shared background and an understanding of what it was like to move from one's home country to the United States. Most immigrants, when they arrive in America, meet up with family or friends who have already moved to the States, and they move into neighborhoods (usually in cities) that are almost entirely of one ethnicity. Immigrant groups traditionally find comfort in a new country by surrounding themselves with people of their own culture. "Immigrants live in neighborhoods very similar to those of native-born in the same racial or ethnic group," say educational sociologists Xue Lan Rong and Judith Preissle, who also claim that immigrant neighborhoods may become permanent in cities. "Most newcomers may move on elsewhere after the initial settlement and adjustment period; however, the next cohort of newcomers from the same race-ethnicity and nationality groups come to fill the vacancies."[11] This often creates long-standing neighborhoods "owned" by a certain ethnicity, giving ethnic gangs the beginnings of a turf to call their own.

Common cultural experiences, language, and living near one another may build a foundation for ethnic gangs, but they do not, in themselves, create gangs. Other social factors are almost always present when gangs form. In particular, the experience of hostility or discrimination from different ethnic groups is believed to lead to the development of gangs as a way for members to stand up for themselves. Part of the process of gang formation, say criminologists Malcolm W. Klein and Cheryl L. Maxson, "includes the gang members' coming to view themselves as the victims of oppression, the unfair targets of racism, inequality, and suppression."[12] Such a sense of interracial opposition existed among European immigrant gangs of the 1800s, and it continued after the source of American immigration shifted from Europe to South America and Asia during the 1900s. As these new immigrant groups swept into the West Coast and Southwest, cities in states like California and Texas became new hotspots for immigrant populations, interracial tension, and the formation of new, mostly ethnic, gangs.

Gangs and Racial Violence

By the 1950s Asian and, especially, Hispanic immigrants were the overwhelming newcomers to America's population. Much like their European forerunners, these immigrants moved in near family and friends in American neighborhoods and bonded together through shared language and ethnic heritage. Gangs quickly formed among these immigrant groups, much as they did among the European immigrants of previous eras. This pointed to a possible need for immigrants to unite against an American culture that did not receive them openly.

Today's Asian gangs, which make up about 7 percent of all gangs in America, are composed of various nationalities, including Chinese, Japanese, Vietnamese, Korean, and Filipino immigrants. Among the largest of these gangs are the Asian Boyz, with members in fourteen states, and the Tiny Rascal Gangsters, a large network of Asian gangs in the Southwest, New England, and along the West Coast. In spite of their differences in ethnic heritage and even language, Asian immigrants seem to bond readily into gangs, suggesting that they perceive hostility from American society against Asians in general. "Members of one Asian ethnic group are often mistaken for being members of

Los Angeles emergency medics give medical aid to gang victims of Hispanic gang violence. Hispanic gangs fight one another more than they fight any other ethnic group.

other Asian ethnic groups," says Angelo N. Ancheta, a civil rights and immigration law professor. "Overt racism is still a serious problem for Asian Americans, just as it has been for African Americans and other racial minorities."[13] Widespread racial hostility from an exclusive, white cultural majority could lead to an "Asians-versus-whites" mentality, and this may be what causes multicultural Asian gangs to form.

Gangs of Hispanic immigrants, such as the Latin Kings in Chicago and New York and the Norteños and Sureños of the West Coast, present a somewhat different picture. They seem to lack a general "Hispanics-versus-whites" mentality. Rather than unifying as a broad ethnic group in a move against general anti-Hispanic feelings in America, many Hispanic gangs develop their chief rivalries not with white people but with other Hispanic groups, often those who have immigrated from different Central or South American countries. "Most Hispanic gang violence is *intraracial*—that is, directed against other Hispanics,"[14] say criminologists Robert M. Regoli, John D. Hewitt, and Matt DeLisi. Hispanic gangs are today the largest ethnic gang group in America, forming about half of all the country's gangs, and they also have the highest rate of violence within their own ethnicity. Hispanic gangs fight one another more than they fight any other ethnic group. About 80 percent of Hispanic gang violence is directed at other Hispanics. This suggests that if gangs do form in part to protect their members from attacks by outsiders, it is not necessarily mainstream American society they feel threatened by. Examples of unity among Asian groups and rivalry among Hispanic groups suggest that immigrants' ethnicity alone may not be the main reason driving the formation of gangs or holding them together.

Immigration also is not the only social situation that seems to give rise to gangs. Only a fraction of all immigrants to America during any time period have actually become gang members. Most find other ways to cope with life in a new country. Not all gangs consist of immigrant groups, either. After Hispanic gangs, black gangs make up the second-largest ethnic gang group in America. About 35 percent of all American gang members belong to black gangs. The remaining 9 percent are in white gangs, many of which have "white supremacist" attitudes and believe that the white race is superior to other races. Members of these latter gangs often refer to themselves as skinheads because they shave off their hair. Most white gangs arise in poor, rural areas. Their members tend to have little hope of improving their financial or social status in the future and blame others—especially minority cultures—for their underprivileged lifestyle.

Because about 44 percent of the nation's total gang population consists of African American and white gangs, not immigrants, the stressful experience of moving to a new country clearly is not the only factor that contributes to the formation of gangs. Gangs do not arise based on race or national origin alone. "Gangs exist in all ethnic categories," says Catherine H. Conly, a consultant for the National Institute of Justice, adding that gangs do not always group by ethnicity. "In some cities, such as Los Angeles and Chicago, gangs are usually racially or ethnically segregated. . . . In other locations, such as Miami, gangs are racially mixed."[15] Clearly, cultural factors other than race have a role in the formation of gangs.

Gangs and Youth

Age is one of the most significant factors that contribute to the phenomenon of gangs. Youth and an attraction to gangs go hand in hand. Throughout the long history of gangs across generations and ethnic cultures, the average age of gang members has remained a steady factor. The gang population traditionally has drawn from teenagers and young adults. Although gang members have ranged from as young as eight years old to their mid-fifties or older, the majority of people who have belonged to American gangs typically have been between the ages of twelve and twenty-four. In fact, the gang problem in America is often referred to specifically as a *youth* gang problem, because most gang members are in their teens and early twenties. According to social ecology professor James Diego Vigil, "It is unavoidably clear that gangs constitute one of the most important urban youth issues in the United States today."[16] The fact that gangs seem to appeal so strongly to the young has led gang researchers to examine what social factors may cause teens and young adults to turn to the gang lifestyle and what these young members look for when they join a gang.

Gang researchers believe that feeling distanced from one's own family may spur young people to seek out gangs. "The most frequently cited reason for people joining gangs is to belong,"[17] says criminal justice expert Kären M. Hess. A supportive and loving family with strong adult role models is a human necessity. Unfortunately, family upheaval is common in America, especially in the environment of the inner city, where most gangs form. Data from the U.S. Census Bureau in 2006 showed that there were about 13 million single-parent families in the country, and about 10 million of those were single-mother families. This means that millions of American children are growing up in fatherless homes with single, working mothers struggling to support their families. Some of these mothers have little time to oversee the activities of their children. While not all gang members come from so-called broken homes, and not all kids from broken homes join gangs, a lack of parental involvement is a risk factor for gang membership. It is estimated that from 50 to 85 percent of America's gang members lived in a broken home before they joined a gang. Without parental supervision, kids and teens tend to spend most of their free time with friends instead of at home. Especially in inner-city environments, kids may hang out on city streets already populated with gangs and become familiar with "gang family" life at an early age. Those who receive little attention or support at home might envy what they see as a brotherhood or sisterhood in the

In some areas gangs are ethnically segregated while gangs in places such as Miami, Florida, and Southern California are racially mixed.

gang lifestyle. "The close ties of gang members are a major motive for membership,"[18] says Hess.

FAMILY MATTERS

"We're family, you know? We ain't got nothing but this gang."— Member, North Side Mafia of Denver, Colorado.

Quoted in "Mile High Killers," *Gangland Season 4*, DVD, produced by Steven Feinartz and Tracy Ullman, A&E Home Video, 2009.

A lack of parental supervision sometimes also means a lack of parental love and attention as well as family safety and security. Abuse and neglect are common factors in the home life of many kids and teens who become gang members. They may turn to gang life as a response to a lack of love and support at home. Stanley "Tookie" Williams, who cofounded the Los Angeles Crips gang in the 1970s and was executed by the state in 2005 for gang-related crimes, wrote about his own fatherless childhood and how it influenced him as he grew up. "I attempted to step into the male position vacated by my father," he wrote. "I believed I was grown, making it impossible for any male to substitute for a father figure." He described beatings he received from his mother as a child and went on to tell how he eventually turned to the streets: "I just found the streets to be more interesting than being at home. . . . It felt liberating to be able to face the street adventures and to make my own decisions about what I should do."[19] Williams's story may reflect similar experiences of gang members who have felt separated from or shunned by their own families.

Among immigrants, there is often an extra layer of separation between kids and their parents as kids try to blend into the environment and values of American society. Their parents, meanwhile, may have religious and social values that conflict with American ways. This sometimes leads to fights between parents and children, and it makes some newly immigrated kids and teens feel ostracized by their parents and families. These young people may be especially attracted to gang culture, which they might see as a surrogate or stand-in family.

How a Gang Lifestyle Is Learned

The American school system also may have a role in turning young people toward gangs. Because neighborhood schools mirror the social environment of the larger community, school-aged kids and teens of the same ethnicity often tend to hang out together at school, forming cliques and avoiding other groups. Some kids have older siblings, cousins, or other family members who are involved in gangs. These kids, already familiar with the gang lifestyle, then bring gang beliefs into their own clique or group within their school. In this way, schools may become a training ground for future gang members, especially among students who feel ignored by their families at home and shunned by the school's teachers and administrators, something that can happen to students whose grades are low and who do not participate in sports teams, academic or social clubs, or other traditional American student pastimes. "Youths who are weakly (or not at all) tethered to home and school have weakened ties to society's conventional institutions and values,"[20] says Vigil. In many cases, the only role models who seem to care about such kids and teens are gang members. "Most youths who become gangsters have had no positive adult role models in their lives," says criminologist Lewis Yablonsky. "The role models they have are fathers, older brothers, and uncles who have been involved in the drug and gang scene."[21] Some of these kids tend to spend much of their time hanging out on the streets, often with gang-related friends.

Unfortunately, in cities that are overrun with gangs, the streets are not safe places to be. Violence between gangs, one of the longest-standing characteristics of the gang problem in America, makes it dangerous to walk through some neighborhoods alone. Fights break out among rival gangs for little or no reason, and kids and teens who have to navigate these neighborhoods feel safer in groups. The larger and fiercer the group, the safer a young person may feel. Safety in numbers is another leading reason why young people in cities feel the need to join

Safety in numbers and the need for social allies are just two of the reasons young people join gangs.

a gang. The gang provides a network of street allies in a dangerous and violent environment.

Many, if not most, gang members say that gangs provide them with a loyal and protective family. If this is true, however, it is a family dominated by men. Women and girls, long considered the nurturers among the human population, do not hold central roles in most of America's gangs. This suggests that the "family ties" most gang members claim to have found may have less to do with love, attachment, and traditional family than with a need to create a male-centered, violent world. Gangs are not just substitutes for inner-city families that have failed to love and nurture their kids, because girls and women are often excluded from the gang version of family altogether, or mistreated and disrespected within that family.

The Gender Gap in Gangs

Of approximately 1 million gang members in the United States today, police gang experts believe that only about 10 percent of them are female, although many researchers think these estimates may be too low. "[Girls'] participation in gangs is more widespread than has typically been believed,"[22] says gang sociologist Jody Miller. Girls and young women certainly take an active part in gang life in America. Yet, most gangs have always been male centered. Some major gangs in the United States today, including most outlaw motorcycle gangs, do not allow women to become members at all, although they may let women associate with them as girlfriends or helpers of male gang members. A few gangs, such as the Hispanic gang Mara Salvatrucha 13 (also known as MS-13), are true mixed-gender

Gangsta Girls

Girl gangs are one of the least understood aspects of the gang phenomenon. Female gang members are far outnumbered by males and are believed to have less status in gangs. Few all-girl gangs are known, typically operating as female branches of larger male gangs: The Norteñas, for example, are affiliated with the male Norteños gang, and the Cripettes are the female version of the Crips gang. Most female gangsters, however, see themselves as independent and capable criminals. Many participate in the fistfight gang initiation ritual called a jump-in, and most are willing to fight and kill for the gang and to play important roles in the drug trade or other illegal activities. Tradition- ally, the court system has given lighter punishments to female gang members convicted of crimes, but as their deeds become more violent and resemble the actions of males, gang women are receiving harsher sentences in court. Those who serve time in prison find a perfect environment there for an all-women gang; they no longer have to compete with men for control and power. In women's prisons, girl gangs can freely reign. According to the National Gang Center, girl gangsters have a presence both in prison and on the streets. Police jurisdictions nationwide, both in cities and towns, report that about half of the gangs in their areas now have female members.

groups that allow girls to become full-fledged members with the same gang privileges and responsibilities that male members have. The majority of gangs, however, are male-dominated and at best have girls-only branches, which often consist of sisters and girlfriends of the male gang members and who generally follow the orders of the men—for example, the Hispanic Norteños gang with its female branch, the Norteñas. Some gangs include women not as true members but as employees, such as in drug and prostitution rings.

Across gang culture, girls and women are rarely given the same respect in the gang that males receive. Female gang members often assist the males, taking orders but rarely having a say in what the gang plans or does. In some gangs, female associates even wear clothing that states they are the "property" of the gang or of a particular gang member. The role of women in some gangs includes doing sexual favors for the men. Hess says women gangsters "are often drug dependent and physically abused."[23] Ironically, abuse at home is actually what makes many girls and women turn to gangs in the first place, says Marc Lacey, a journalist for the *New York Times*. "Gangs often continue the abuse," he says, "offering what proves to be an unpredictable mix of affection and aggression."[24] If the search for family ties is really what drives gangs together, then the surrogate family relationship is not, at least for women, a way to fulfill the need for love and acceptance that traditional families provide, and young women who affiliate with gangs usually do not stay long. "Girls' gang involvement tends to be of shorter duration than boys'," says Miller, "with girls' peak gang involvement around eighth or ninth grades,"[25] whereas males often stay in gangs until well into their twenties or later. The gang-as-family motivation for gang membership does not seem to hold up for most young women.

Although in recent years, a few girls-only gangs have formed independently of male gangs in America, gangs remain, as they have always been, a phenomenon mostly created among and dominated by males. Many researchers think one reason for this lies in a fourth cultural factor that could be perhaps the most important thing driving gangs together, surpassing even the importance of ethnicity, age, and gender. That factor is poverty.

Gangs and Economic Opportunity

Perhaps the strongest predictor of gang formation in a community is the overall economic status of its residents. The poorer the neighborhood or area, the more likely that gangs will form within it. This is one characteristic that seems to have been common among most if not all gangs in America throughout the nation's history. Regardless of the ethnicity, immigrant status, age, or gender of their members, gangs almost always form in impoverished areas, places where living conditions are unpleasant and where good jobs and a good education seem out of reach. A sense of hopelessness and pointlessness, of having been forgotten or snubbed by the rest of America, is overwhelming in such places. In cities, these run-down neighborhoods are known as slums, and they are the primary breeding ground for gangs. "If the spread of gangs cannot be accounted for solely by the underclass phenomenon, it is nevertheless the case that the vast majority of gangs in cities throughout the country arise among less affluent youth,"[26] says sociologist James F. Short.

FALSE LOYALTY

"When they get in trouble, they will inform on each other. And so all the things that they kind of grow up saying, you know, 'we're united, we're together,'" you know, none of those things hold."— Mitch Morrissey, district attorney, Denver, Colorado.

Quoted in "Mile High Killers," *Gangland Season 4*, DVD, produced by Steven Feinartz and Tracy Ullman, A&E Home Video, 2009.

Poverty could be the common element that ties together all the other cultural factors of gangs. If people living in poor neighborhoods can find work at all, it may be in undesirable, low-paying jobs with few or no benefits—as convenience store clerks or waitresses in neighborhood diners, for example, or as menial laborers such as janitors or gas station attendants. Immigrants, particularly those who do not speak English, often find it difficult to get a job that pays high wages. To make ends meet,

Gangs Behind Bars

City streets are home to a large majority of gangs in the United States, but a growing portion of the gang population dwells in the prison system. Nearly 150,000 of the country's gang members are in prison, although not all belonged to street gangs before their convictions. Prison itself seems to intensify the major risk factors for street gang membership—impoverished living conditions, feelings of hopelessness, absence of loved ones and social support systems, and fear of being a victim of gang violence. There is tremendous pressure on inmates to join a gang for companionship and protection. Prison gangs are often considered survival mechanisms for prisoners.

Prison gangs, like street gangs, are often defined by race or ethnicity. Major U.S. prison gangs include the Mexican Mafia, the Aryan Brotherhood, Nuestra Familia, the Texas Syndicate, and the Black Guerrilla Family. Members of prison gangs may also be members of separate street gangs, and many prison gangs have developed street-gang branches or alliances with street gangs. But the worst dangers of prison gangs are within prison walls, where they cause riots, commit murders, and make prison a brutal and dangerous place.

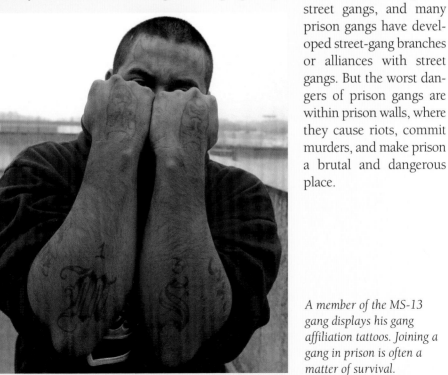

A member of the MS-13 gang displays his gang affiliation tattoos. Joining a gang in prison is often a matter of survival.

Extreme poverty could be the common element that ties together all other cultural factors of gangs.

adults raising families in poverty-stricken areas may have to work at multiple low-paying jobs, which means that children and teens are often left unsupervised at home and more susceptible to gang influence on the streets. The stress of never having enough money can make some families hostile, and an abusive home environment in turn forces some young people into a gang lifestyle as well.

People living in impoverished communities often feel shunned by an American system that they feel gives them few or no opportunities to improve their status in society. "Basically," says Vigil, "the street gang is an outcome of marginalization, that is, the relegation of certain persons or groups to the fringes of society, where social and economic conditions result in powerlessness."[27] Young men, in particular, crave the chance to be successful, have good-paying jobs, support themselves and their families, and be respected figures in their communities. If gangs can meet some of these needs, it may explain why the gang culture is so male-dominated.

Living in poverty is considered the single strongest driving force behind the formation of gangs in America and is also the most significant factor that gangs throughout American history have had in common. The harsh realities of life in a desperately poor neighborhood often remain constant over time. The slum neighborhoods of American cities today may be home to different ethnic populations than they were in the 1800s, but daily life in these neighborhoods has changed surprisingly little. Decades may pass, but in slums, it is always "business as usual." And for poor and underprivileged inner-city populations, a business is, in fact, what many gangs have become.

CHAPTER 3

GANGS AS BUSINESSES

Gangs may appeal to young people because they provide—or promise to provide—for them the way their parents cannot. A gang often becomes its members' lifeline for the basic human needs of food, a place to live, and an income with which to buy clothes and other necessities. Seeking out a new type of family for material support may be what drives young members into the gang lifestyle at first. Those who stick around into adulthood may do so because the gang is their only source of income. Most gangs are not just groups that hang out together for friendship and family. They are also a kind of business that participates in illegal activities to make money. Crime may be the only type of employment that many gang members think is available to them. "Sadly, education does not provide the same financial rewards for lower-income youth as it does for youth in middle-income groups," say social development researchers Ian Bannon and Maria C. Corriea. "Class, race, and gender barriers, combined with limited social capital, hinder their employment opportunities."[28]

Gangs are more than just social clubs of people who live in the same neighborhood and share the same background. The very definition of a gang, according to the U.S. Department of Justice, is a group whose activities include crime, and most types of crimes that gangs commit are done for profit, either to make money for the gang directly or to protect its moneymaking methods. Crime is a business for gangs, no matter what their ethnicity or where they operate. "[Gang members] believe the profits from crime are worth the risk of punishment," says Larry Siegel. "It may be their only significant chance for gain or profit."[29] Greed, in fact, may be one of the strongest characteristics of gangs. They need or want money, and most gangs and their members seem willing to do almost anything to get it.

Crime for Profit

Crime is notorious among gangs. It is the main reason they are dreaded and feared in their own communities. Most of them operate with no regard for the law, and they commit a wide range of crimes on a daily and nightly basis to bring profit to the gang. Popular gang crimes have always included burglary and theft. It is common practice in many cities for gang members to rob stores, steal merchandise, or mug strangers in order to take their cash and other valuables. A main commodity for gangster thieves is vehicles. In the gang world, a fancy, expensive car is a valuable item that can be resold or even kept by the gang to improve its status among rival gangs, but almost any vehicle can be targeted. Gangs frequently break into cars to take valuable items such as stereo systems, or they may steal the entire

Many gangs start car theft rings as businesses.

car to break it down into parts they can resell. Robbery of all kinds is one of the oldest ways gangs have made money.

Other criminal moneymaking schemes are popular among gangs, too. At least as early as the 1920s, when the Italian Mafia ruled the gang world in big cities like Chicago and New York, gangsters collected "taxes" from people, sometimes in return for protecting a business from criminals and rival gangs and sometimes just for the privilege of using a particular service or going to a certain place. Many of today's gangs also demand taxes from business owners, street vendors, and even taxi drivers who operate in the gang's neighborhood. Those who do not pay the tax may get bullied and harassed, their businesses may be vandalized, and their customers may be chased away by the gang. In many cities, large gangs also demand such taxes from smaller gangs, and any that refuse to pay become targets of gang violence. Cities with gang populations have reported that fear of gangs was an "'immediate,' daily experience for people who lived in lower-income neighborhoods where gangs were more prevalent and dangerous," says James C. Howell, a senior research associate with the National Youth Gang Center. "In the most gang-ridden areas," he says, "many residents reported having avoided gang areas because they were afraid of gangs and criminal victimization."[30]

In addition to stealing things and collecting taxes, many gangs also run crime rings, or associations that collectively commit a type of crime in order to make a profit. Some gangs are involved in the prostitution industry, for example, employing women and teenage girls to sell sex to strangers. Prostitutes give their profits back to the gang in exchange for a salary or other payment, perhaps in the form of food and a place to live. Outlaw motorcycle gangs are notorious for making money from prostitution. "Motorcycle gangs are male dominated and women are treated as property," says gang researcher Donnie Harris. Women who are associated with these gangs are often "forced into prostitution," Harris says, and "often put to work in strip clubs and must give earnings to the gang."[31]

By far the most profitable crime among today's gangs, however, is the selling of illegal items—especially drugs. Drugs and gangs nearly always go hand in hand. Virtually every major gang on the streets of America's cities and towns is involved in the drug trade. Most have a particular drug of choice, such as crack cocaine, heroin, or methamphetamine, but a single gang may deal in multiple kinds of drugs. Many gangs also sell weapons, such as automatic rifles, that are not easy to find and rarely legal to buy. Because potential customers have few sources from which to obtain illegal items like weapons and drugs, gangs can charge a lot of money for this merchandise, and they usually receive their asking price.

ALL IN A DAY'S WORK

"Business is business. Money is money. Brotherhood's a hoax."—Jimmy DeGregorio, former member of the Pagans motorcycle gang.

Quoted in "Devil's Fire," *Gangland, Season 4*, DVD, produced by Steven Feinartz and Tracy Ullman, A&E Home Video, 2009.

Gang researchers think that some gangs form specifically for the purpose of carrying out illegal commerce, not for social reasons the way other gangs might. Such "opportunistic gangs," as political science researcher Deborah Lamm Weisel calls them, "are organized primarily for the purpose of distributing drugs," and they "operate as business organizations primarily to engage in criminal activities." Weisel says that the financial goals are the most important focus of such gangs: "The organization is motivated by profits and market control . . . [and] loyalty of individuals to the gang is related to economic reasons."[32]

One important fact of illegal gang business is that gangster criminals rarely if ever act alone. Whether they are stealing cars, holding up convenience stores, monitoring prostitutes on the streets, or selling drugs and guns, gang members are almost always operating as part of a larger organization. Gang crime is a form of organized crime; that is, a group of people works together to commit or carry out crime to make money, and they

Law enforcement officials display weapons confiscated from local gangs. Many gangs sell weapons that are hard to get, such as automatic weapons.

all pool their profits for the benefit of the group. In many gangs, the entire arrangement of membership is based on this one goal.

Gangs as Business Operations

The very way gangs are structured supports the fact that most function as a sort of business enterprise for their members. Some of the nation's oldest and most successful gangs, including the Italian Mafia, the mostly African American Vice Lord Nation, and the Black Guerrilla Family, have been around for decades and resemble legitimate businesses in many ways. Like almost any business, most gangs are hierarchies, organizations that have different levels of status and power for their members. The newer, less experienced members are at the bottom of a gang's status scale, and at the top of the hierarchy are the gang members with the most status, the ones who make decisions for the gang and tell the rest of the organization what to do. Some gangs, such as the Italian Mafia, even call their leaders bosses the way most companies do in the corporate world, supporting the argument that many gangs think of themselves as businesses, even if their industry is crime.

As in the world of legitimate business, gang members continuously try to gain more power and a higher status in the organization, a process known as climbing the ranks. Gang members seek respect and status in the gang, and the way to get it is to "put in work." Among gangsters, "work" means doing something, usually an illegal act, for the benefit of the gang, and it can range from stealing money or merchandise to selling drugs to beating up or killing a member of a rival gang. Gang members seek money, rewards, and praise from the organization. Much the way successful workers in the business world get raises and promotions, gang members who work hard are able to rise in wealth and power. "Gangs are corporations, literally," says education analyst Anne Turnbaugh Lockwood, "with individuals filtering through the ranks and promoted to higher positions for superior accomplishments and contributions to the group."[33]

The businesslike structure and the moneymaking priorities of gangs date back at least to the 1920s and the era of Prohibition, when Mafia mobsters ran large, tightly organized criminal businesses that competed with each other and with other gangs for wealth. Prohibition gangs were businesses to the extent that everything they did, even murdering people, was done in an efficient and businesslike manner. "A Mafia family was more than just a street gang," says Reppetto. "It was a commercial enterprise, and it had to be run that way."[34]

Prohibition-era gangs gave rise to modern gangs that still operate with the goal of conducting business to make money.

Many gang experts, however, believe that today's gangs are not nearly as businesslike as their 1920s predecessors. Some gangs do have a precise leadership structure, with officers such as a president, vice president, treasurer, and sergeant at arms (a person in charge of keeping order in the gang, often through violence). Many black gangs, such as the Vice Lords and the Black P. Stone Nation gang, as well as the outlaw motorcycle gang the Hells Angels, are structured this way, and the leaders keep tight control over the business operations of the entire gang. Many other gangs, however, have a more lateral leadership, in which a panel or a board of leaders rather than one particular president or boss makes decisions for the gang. This is a more common structure among fast-growing Hispanic gangs such as the Los Angeles–based 18th Street gang and Tango Blast in the state of Texas, neither of which closely resembles the organized hierarchy of the Mafia. Sociologist Martín Sánchez Jankowski says that the Hispanic gangs he has studied "tended to downplay the goal of accumulating a great deal of capital. This is not to say that they were not interested in accumulating money, only that they did not emphasize it as much as did the gangs in the East."[35] Without a tight, central structure, gangs tend to grow larger and may become unruly.

Businesses Run Amok

Any large gang, regardless of the way it is organized, runs the risk of getting too big to be governed tightly by its leaders. In fact, the more structure a gang has, the less happy its members often are within it. Gang members become greedy for money and power and may resent being told what to do by the leaders of their gang. When this happens, new gangs tend to splinter off from the original ones to make different gangs, and formerly lower-ranked members then have a chance to become leaders in the new gang. In a ten-year study of major gangs in New York, Boston, and Los Angeles in the 1980s, Jankowski found that when a gang collapsed, "it was either incorporated into the structure of a rival gang (much like a takeover in the business world) or broke into factions that reorganized into a new gang or gangs."[36]

The tendency of large or disorganized gangs to splinter is the cause of many rivalries between gangs, because gang tension is based largely on competition for the criminal profits to be made in a neighborhood shared by multiple gangs. One notorious and decades-old gang rivalry is that between the Black Disciples and the Gangster Disciples of Chicago, both of which splintered off from the Black Gangster Disciples gang in the 1970s and have been fighting each other for dominance of their turf ever since. "Much intergang rivalry, fighting and killing stem from conflict over control of a neighborhood, which represents the cornerstone of the drug business operations for street-level business dealers," explains Felix M. Padilla, a professor of Latin American and Puerto Rican Studies. "The phrase 'control of the neighborhood,'" Padilla says, "stands for gang

Gang Recruiting

Gangs with profitable criminal businesses have long been known to recruit new gang workers, people willing to perform street-level crimes for the gang such as selling drugs to customers or carrying out "hits"—acts of physical punishment or murder—on the gang's enemies. A recent trend in gang recruiting has targeted minors, kids who are under age eighteen and sometimes as young as elementary school. The U.S. legal system generally gives lighter punishments to minors who are caught and convicted of crimes, so the younger the gang-related criminal, the smaller the legal risk for the gang. Gangsters who are kids may receive only community service, limited jail time in a juvenile detention center, or some combination of similar punishments for crimes like burglary and drug trafficking, whereas an adult gang member who commits the same crimes might be sentenced to prison. Even in murder cases, kids under age eighteen are less likely than adults to be sentenced to life in prison without parole. By getting kids to conduct their criminal business, older gang members avoid punishment. In many states, however, including Washington, Arizona, New Jersey, and Nevada, recruiting minors into gangs is against the law. So even if minor gang members commit no crimes, those who recruited them into the gang may go to prison for it.

ownership of territory from which to conduct business activities."[37] Rivalry over business is also a major reason why some gangs spread into new neighborhoods and cities, and even to smaller towns. They are branching into new markets where they can carry out their business ventures with less competition, much the way legal businesses such as restaurant franchises grow and expand when they are successful.

Franchise or False Belief?

Many gangs have no formal structure, no official plan, and no "leader" telling everyone else what to do; these are the fastest-spreading gangs, because there is little authority in the gang to oversee where and how new members are recruited. Most of these types of gangs have "sets," or smaller divisions of the

In 2002 Los Angeles police chief Bernard Parks announced an injunction against the 18th Street gang. The injunction made it illegal for the gang to exist in Los Angeles.

whole. Each set may be active in crime and recruit new members without needing the approval of a gang president or leader. Some gang experts believe that such gangs spread easily outside the borders of their hometowns, home states, and even home countries. A troubling example is Hispanic gangs that now move readily between the United States and Central American countries, gangs such as 18th Street and Mara Salvatrucha 13 that have widespread membership in El Salvador, Honduras, Guatemala, Nicaragua, and the United States. "They have exported their gang culture—learned . . . in the big cities of the United States—to other countries in Central and South America," says *Time* magazine reporter Carmen Gentile, and they are now "re-exporting their influence back to the U.S., moving beyond petty thievery, flashy tattoos and thuggish violence, to drug-trafficking and large-scale extortion."[38] In other words, international gangs tend to adopt the worst criminal and social aspects of each country they operate in. And by straddling national borders, some create criminal channels and networks through which drugs and crime spread easily from place to place. The potential for criminal gangs to spread like this means that they could pose an increasing problem for law enforcement agencies and for law-abiding people in several different countries who fear being victims of ever-spreading gang crime.

Few people dispute that gangs are growing, both in size and number, in the United States, but not all gang experts agree that gangs easily franchise or spread from one city to another. "Gang members move outside the neighborhood—to suburbs or other cities," says Weisel, but they "come back to hang out in the original neighborhood. Only occasionally do these displaced members start a new gang chapter in their new communities."[39] Howell agrees. "Gang migration, if it occurs, generally extends only approximately 100 miles from the city of origin, and rarely further," he says. "Few gangs have the capacity to extend into other regions."[40] Thus, contrary to concerns that the gang problem is growing because existing gangs can spread boundlessly, it is very possible that when gangs appear for the first time in a new community, they are formed on the spot, instead of moving in from a different city.

The Mob Lives On

The Italian Mafia was infamous in the Prohibition era, but it did not die with the downfall of megamobsters like Al Capone. It is still alive and well in today's gang culture. Also known as La Cosa Nostra (LCN), Italian for "this thing of ours," the Italian Mafia currently has about three thousand members in the United States. Though it is not nearly the largest criminal gang in the nation, its serious and sophisticated crimes put it in a different category than most other American gangs. Divided into powerful, wealthy, and well-connected families, including New York City's well-known Gambino, Luchese, and Genovese families,

LCN's criminal activities are highly organized, and LCN masterminds find ingenious ways to shelter themselves from criminal investigations. This makes LCN difficult to prosecute. In addition to common gang crimes like drug sales, prostitution, and murder, LCN is deeply involved in complex, highly profitable crimes like loan sharking, tax fraud, tampering with the stock market, bribing or threatening large businesses for a share of their profits, money laundering, and corruption of elected officials. The FBI considers La Cosa Nostra the leading organized crime threat in the United States today.

Reputed captain of the Genovese crime family Michael Coppola appears in court in 2007 to face charges for a 1977 mob murder.

Many gang researchers also do not believe that most gangs are organized enough to carry out large-scale crimes and dominate whole portions of cities, despite what media reports may claim. "Most youth gangs are not as formidable as these sources would have us believe,"[41] says Howell. The majority of gangs are really quite disorganized, says Chris Mathers, who has worked with gangs as an undercover officer for the Federal Bureau of Investigation (FBI) and the Drug Enforcement Administration (DEA). "Most gangs couldn't put a pound of grass [marijuana] together if you relied on the gang as an entity to do so,"[42] he says. The idea that all American gangs are sophisticated crime organizations may overestimate their criminal capability. Many experts believe that gangs are still merely a social response to tough economic conditions, groups of people clinging to the fringes of mainstream society and making a desperate attempt to earn a living in an environment where other kinds of jobs and financial prospects are scarce. "Gangs have become an important ghetto employer that offers low-level drug dealing opportunities that are certainly not available in the nongang world," says Siegel. "In this uneasy economic climate, gangs flourish."[43]

SCHOOL'S OUT

"You got all these people telling us to get an education—I'm making thousands of dollars each month. Why do I need to go to school?"—Michael, a gang member in Chicago, Illinois.

Quoted in Sudhir Venkatesh, "The Gang Tax," *New York Times* Freakonomics blog, Opinion, April 8, 2008. http://freakonomics.blogs.nytimes.com/2008/04/08/the-gang-tax/.

Still, the image of gangs as the criminal moneymakers of America is not entirely undeserved. "In some cities, gangs have exercised 'ruthless control' of areas for decades,"[44] says criminal justice professor John Hagedorn. The opportunity, the expectation, and even the need for gangs to commit crime are characteristics shared by virtually every group that is classified as a gang. Gangs may rise out of the poverty and misery of under-privileged living conditions, but their widespread criminal mindset has turned them into a worrisome problem for police and communities. "Poverty and slums . . . have become an intractable reality," says Hagedorn, "spawning despair and angry young men."[45] Gangs are a growing counterculture, a group whose values and lifestyle differ from the rest of America. Gangs are real, and so are their crimes. The way society and especially the legal system responds to them is one of the most important issues facing modern-day America.

CHAPTER 4

GANGS AND THE LEGAL SYSTEM

Gangs are in the business of crime. The criminal nature of their activity is the main thing that divides gangs from other groups such as clubs or companies. Not all gangs commit the same numbers or types of crimes, but on the whole, they are involved in the drug trade, prostitution, extortion (forcing) of money from nongang citizens and businesses in their neighborhoods, burglary and theft, the sale of illegal weapons, and other unlawful doings. Gangs take part in a variety of criminal pursuits, and not all gangs specialize in the same illegal activities. There is one kind of crime, however, that virtually all gangs in modern America have in common: violence. Gangs fight and gangs kill. This characteristic, more than any other, defines modern gangs and makes the rest of society fear them.

Killing Without Targets

Violence is the most pressing issue that gangs create. Gang members tend to be territorial and fiercely loyal to their own gang. At the same time, gangs view each other as rivals competing for the same area of a neighborhood, the same share of criminal income, or the same power and influence in their community. Gangs frequently challenge one another, and those challenges can be dangerously violent. Most gang members see it as their duty to defend the gang against rivals, and they do so with no regard for innocent people who literally get caught in the cross fire of their violence.

Gang fighting is nothing new. Gangs of earlier eras had rivalries just like the gangs of today. Their fights often took the

Authorities carry away a Washington, D.C., drive-by shooting victim. Drive-by shootings have turned neighborhoods into killing grounds.

form of a rumble, a large, preplanned skirmish in which two or more gangs would fight with fists and knives. Rumbles were huge brawls that resulted in serious, often fatal, injuries among participants, and they worried citizens and police. But for non-gang society, gang violence in the form of a rumble was easy to avoid—people just stayed away from the scene of the fight.

By the early 1900s gangs had become more organized and their violence took a new turn. Rather than group rumbles in which gangs fought hand to hand, gangsters began targeting just one or a few specific members of rival gangs to execute. These murders were called hits, usually carried out by assassins called hit men. Most victims of hit men were killed with guns, often shot from within a passing car. The drive-by style of gang shooting is believed to have been invented by the notorious Mafia gangster Al Capone, and it forever changed the way gang fights were carried out. To this day, gangster killers frequently roam the streets in vehicles, and any rival gang member could be a target of a shooting, anywhere, anytime.

The modern shooting style of gang murder puts the public at serious risk of injury from gang violence. Gang shootings can turn city streets, parking lots, and crowded places like shopping malls into instant war zones where bullets fly with no regard for anyone's safety. "In the maniacal fray into 'enemy territory' of a drive-by, gang members inaccurately [shoot] and kill as many innocent people as the enemy gangsters they are attempting to kill,"[46] says Yablonsky. Gang violence becomes even more dangerous when gangsters acquire automatic rifles, machine gun–style weapons that launch bullets far more rapidly than single-shot handguns can. Gang shooters increasingly prefer automatic assault weapons, and they spray bullets in public areas with disastrous results. Many victims of gang shootings have no gang involvement at all. "Only about 50 percent of gang-related murders hit the target of enemy gangsters," says Yablonsky. "The other 50 percent of victims of drive-bys and street violence are innocent children and adults who happen to be in the wrong place at the wrong time."[47] When gang shootouts wound or kill innocent people, outraged citizens of a community usually begin to demand that police do something to rid their town or city of its gang problems.

The Worst of All Gangs

Mara Salvatrucha 13, or MS-13, is widely considered the most dangerous gang in the United States. Its tactics are fearful and its violence boundless. It began in Los Angeles in the 1980s among immigrants from the Central American country of El Salvador, a nation troubled by civil war. Because of civil war at home, most Salvadorans had been trained in war tactics and weapons use, and in Los Angeles, these immigrants banded together into a deadly gang. MS-13 uses a military fighting style with lookouts and automatic guns, and many members use large-bladed knives called machetes in hand-to-hand combat. Loosely structured and lacking strong central leadership, the gang has branched readily into new places and now exists in a majority of U.S. states. In a controversial effort to control the spread of MS-13, the U.S. legal system has deported some of the gang's members back to Central America, where they have spread their Americanized gang tactics and violence to smaller nations unprepared to deal with them. MS-13's vicious, terrorizing tactics include slashing victims to death with machetes. And the gang is growing faster than any in United States history. MS-13 is considered the worst street gang the country has ever seen, and it has done more than any other group to make American society fear modern gangs and what they have—and could—become.

Newark, New Jersey, police director Garry McCarthy reveals the photos of six MS-13 affiliated gang members indicted on murder, attempted murder, robbery, and weapons offenses related to the killing of three college students in Newark in August 2007.

Cross-Country Gangs

Communities that turn to law enforcement for protection against gangs usually want to see quick results. Getting gang crime and violence under control is more difficult than most people realize, however, in part because gangs and their activities often spread beyond the police jurisdiction of a single community. The extent to which gangs actually migrate from place to place or set up satellite gang groups in different cities, states, and countries is debatable, but many gangs do expand their illegal business contacts and tap into a criminal network that stretches out of their city, state, or even out of the country, often making it a challenge for local police to fully contain a gang and its activities. Hispanic gangs, for example, often have a role in the smuggling of illegal drugs such as heroin and cocaine from Mexico and South America into the United States. Most gang researchers believe few U.S. gangs have enough organization or control over their members to actually *operate* the kind of drug cartel, or group of drug smuggling organizations, that exists in Mexico and South America, but many U.S. gangs do have a *partnership* with drug cartels. The cartels supply the drugs, while multiple U.S.-based gangs help move drugs across the national border and into American cities. "One gang, before being stopped by federal authorities, had a cocaine distribution that stretched across five states,"[48] says youth violence researcher Elizabeth Kandel Englander. Getting control over such a spread-out gang requires cooperation and communication among many different police forces, local, state, and national, often making it a long and difficult process to address gang crime.

Gangs straddle not just the country's southern border in states like California, Arizona, New Mexico, and Texas, but also the border between Canada and the United States, especially where the Canadian provinces of Quebec and Ontario meet Michigan and New York. The Canada–United States border is common territory for outlaw motorcycle gangs such as the Hells Angels, the Outlaws, and the Bandidos. These gangs are mostly nomadic criminal groups that ride their motorcycles from city to city and cross readily into Canada and back. Much of the smuggling across Canadian borders involves firearms. According to the Criminal Intelligence Service of Canada (CISC) in its 2007 annual report on organized crime, "Smuggled firearms that cross the land border from the United States are a significant source of illegal firearms due in part to its geographic proximity and less restrictive gun control regulations."[49] Drugs are also smuggled regularly between the United States and Canada.

It is well known that gangs pass contraband, or illegal items, across state and national borders, but it is hard to catch them in the act, complicating law enforcement's response to gangs and their crimes. Patrolling national borders is notoriously difficult. "A number of land border areas are particularly attractive" for smugglers, says the CISC, "due to their often rough and remote geographical nature."[50] The ability of some gangs to carry their illegal activities across borders, or to collaborate with gangs that do, is a main reason why gangs are hard for police to control. Law enforcement officers in one city or state cannot patrol the entire country, and even national security agencies such as the FBI and the DEA find that the widespread nature of the gang problem makes it difficult to contain, especially since American law enforcement cannot control what happens in other countries.

SOMETHING TO BE PROUD OF

"Respect, power, and pride. That's why I joined the gang."—Former member, North Side Mafia of Denver, Colorado.

Quoted in "Mile High Killers," *Gangland, Season 4*, DVD, produced by Steven Feinartz and Tracy Ullman, A&E Home Video, 2009.

Fortunately, not all gangs run international crime rings. "Only a small number of organized crime groups are capable of operating elaborate criminal operations," says the CISC. "A significantly larger proportion of crime groups are distributors of contraband across the country, but are generally not capable of large-scale importation of contraband." However, the CISC says, the distributors of contraband "tend to be more visible to both

A U.S. Bureau of Alcohol, Tobacco, Firearms, and Explosives display shows confiscated weapons obtained from operations to combat smuggling along the U.S.-Mexico border.

law enforcement and the public than more sophisticated criminal groups."[51] In other words, while the most powerful gangs may be the best organized ones, such gangs are also very good at avoiding capture. The lower-level gangs operating mainly on the streets are the ones that tend to be noticed by police and take the fall for most gang crime. This pyramid design has long been successful at protecting higher-ranking individuals in groups like the military, and has also become familiar in the world of gangs.

Pyramids of Crime

In a military organization, soldiers are organized according to rank. Those at the highest level make all the battle plans, and those at the lowest level are given orders to carry out. The top officers are protected in this structure, since they are the most knowledgeable and experienced at war. The lives of entry-level soldiers, on the other hand, tend to be more expendable. This is one reason that soldiers try to climb the ranks of the military—more status means more power but also more protection. Many gangs tend to mimic this pyramid structure. Gang members themselves recognize the similarities between their gang and a military group, commonly referring to themselves as soldiers and to their rivalries with other gangs as wars. Kody Scott, a former member of the Los Angeles Crips gang, says his gang was "an exclusive military machine" made up of "seasoned veterans who could be compared to long-range Reconnaissance Patrol Soldiers in Vietnam.... There was nothing else for us but war, war, war."[52]

A military-like gang structure, such as that of the Mexican American gang Nuestra Familia, consists of generals and captains who give orders to street-level soldiers. The leaders of a military-style gang are rarely the ones selling drugs, smuggling contraband, or carrying out hits on rival gangs. These activities are delegated to the newest, often youngest, gang recruits, or soldiers. In a gang with a military-style philosophy, these recruits are the ones most often in the line of fire from other gangs and the ones most likely to get caught for the gang's crimes. Meanwhile, those who organize the gang's crimes often remain untouched, and the gang continuously recruits new soldiers to replace the ones who are lost. Despite the arrests of many of its members, a military-style gang whose leaders are well protected from prosecution may continue to thrive and grow. Such a gang is structured so that "only the leader knows every precise movement of all the gang members, which makes the job of law enforcement difficult," says retired police detective and gang expert Edward Burns. "A gang's methods of operation are designed to resist a knockout blow"[53] such as the arrest of multiple lower-level gang members by law enforcement.

Gangs with a pyramid structure cause frustration for police, who are usually obligated to prove a motive for a crime. Gang members, like military soldiers, view their gang activity as a job—they are just taking orders and doing what they are told. Violent gang crime often has no other motive, and like soldiers, gang members usually have the mentality that their deeds are the work of the gang as a whole, not of them as individuals. A drive-by gang shooting, for instance, is usually done "by the

Members of the Outlaws motorcycle gang sit under arrest at their headquarters. Gangs like these often consist of veterans and are organized like the military.

gang" and "in the name of the gang," so the person who actually pulled the trigger may feel little or no remorse. During the 2010 trial of a St. Paul, Minnesota, gang member convicted of murdering a man from a rival gang, the nineteen-year-old killer told the court, "I think I'm getting too much time for something that was gang-related. He was a gangbanger, too."[54] His comment shows the depersonalized, war-is-war mentality of gang crimes, which seem to have little specific motive at all.

Group Mentality, but Not Group Justice

If most gang crime is really committed for no other reason than for the sake of the gang, the entire gang is at fault for its crimes, and the most logical response would seem to be to hold the entire gang accountable. But this is not the way the U.S. legal system works. Belonging to a gang is not in itself illegal, nor can police target people for arrest just because they belong to a gang that committed a certain crime. Instead, law enforcement agencies must find specific individuals who have broken a law. Police can make arrests based only on probable cause, or a reasonable belief that a specific person committed a specific crime. Learning which gang members are responsible for crimes and apprehending them can be an inefficient and time-consuming process. Because so many crime problems now involve gangs, many police departments have formed gang units to get to know the gangs and gang members in their communities and to deal with gang problems. This has enabled police departments to better understand criminal motivations and to make more gang arrests. And in some areas, this more effective police crackdown on gangs finally seems to be putting limits on gang crime.

Policing America's Gangs

Local and national police forces across the nation conduct frequent gang sweeps, or widespread roundups of serious gang offenders in a community. Hundreds of law enforcement officers take part in such sweeps. They approach a gang territory, taking into custody numerous gang members on whom they have collected enough evidence to get an arrest warrant. Gang sweeps can result in dozens of arrests. A gang may even be crippled if

Gang Graffiti

The presence of graffiti is often the first sign of a gang's presence in a neighborhood. Gangs use graffiti to mark territory, honor fallen members, communicate about events and business transactions, and even challenge other gangs. Graffiti is usually heaviest at the center of a given gang's territory, where the gang brands all visible public surfaces with its name and symbols. Toward the edges of a gang's territory, though, its graffiti is often challenged. Gangs vying for the same turf often insult each other by writing over graffiti, writing a rival gang's name or symbols upside down, or showing its name split in half. A graffiti insult is a serious offense in the gang world and can set off a killing spree, but graffiti can also serve positive purposes. Police use it to track which gangs are claiming which territories and which are at odds with each other, for example, and some graffiti, especially that of Hispanic gangs, is often artistically beautiful. For Carlos Sanchez, a former gang member who now owns a California art gallery, his artistic talent, which was once confined to gang graffiti, has been a saving grace. "Art can heal," he says. Graffiti expresses "what we can't show in words."

Quoted in Sandra T. Molina, "Former Gang Members Show How Art Changed Their Lives in New Whittier Art Gallery Exhibit," *Whittier (CA) Daily News*, March 20, 2010. www.whittierdailynews.com/news/ci_147 16916#ixzz0jsIpzzhJ.

Graffiti painted by the Crips and the Bloods in Anchorage, Alaska, proves that both gangs claim the territory.

its most powerful members are apprehended, tried, and sentenced to prison. This police tactic is considered one of the most effective ways to subdue gang activity in a community.

ONLY TWO WAYS OUT

"You're not gonna prosper out of being a gang member. There's only two roads you're gonna go. I bless God that I'm not six feet under, and I bless God that I'm not doing 25 to life today."—Jesse Marin, former member of the Logan Heights gang of San Diego, California.

Quoted in "The Assassins," *Gangland, Season 4*, DVD, produced by Steven Feinartz and Tracy Ullman, A&E Home Video, 2009.

Despite evidence that they work to curb gang crime, however, police sweeps may be only a temporary solution to the gang problem. Gang members who are sent to prison often serve just a few months or years, and when they are released, they have criminal records, making it hard for them to get a good job outside of the gang. With nowhere else to go and no other way to make a living, most gang members return to gang life as soon as they have served their time in prison. Jail time does nothing to turn most gang members' lives around. Some convicted gangsters even find ways to continue operating their criminal activity from within prison walls. According to the 2005 National Gang Threat Assessment, "Incarcerating gang members has done little to disrupt their activities and, in many ways, has augmented their growth and power inside prisons. High-ranking gang members are often able to exert their influence on the street from within prison."[55]

Some gangs, like the Texas gang Tango Blast Houstone, offer membership only to people who have served time in prison. Tango Blast Houstone is so influential that wannabe members actually go out of their way to meet its prison prerequisite. "We have run across kids that are just trying to commit a crime so they can get into the prison system so they can become Houstone,"[56] says supervisory special agent Brian Ritchie, who leads the FBI's violent crimes and gangs task force in the city of Houston. In the case of Tango Blast Houstone, prison is not seen as a punishment for gang members but rather a means to achieve the goal of gang membership.

Many gang experts believe that arrest and imprisonment are, at best, short-term solutions to the gang problem. Increased police response to gangs and improved tactics for approaching the gang problem means more gang members are being arrested and convicted than ever before, yet even the threat of prison does not seem to deter people from joining gangs. In order to offer true solutions to gang problems, it is necessary for gang experts to fully understand what draws so many people to the gang lifestyle in the first place. Identifying how and why gangs attract members, and ultimately reducing their ability to do so, may be as important in controlling dangerous gang activity as the legal system has been.

PROMOTING GANG LIFE

Gangs are generally considered to be negative forces in society, unlawful organizations that generate violence, crime, and misery. Yet the gang lifestyle has also been revered in American culture for decades, especially in the media, and this has shaped not only the way the nongang population thinks of gangs but the way gang members think of themselves. Through movies and music, America has come to accept gangs, perhaps even to glorify them. The American gangster has become something of an icon, and this could be one explanation of why gangs are growing across the United States even when their overall reputation is negative. There is something about the gang lifestyle and gang values that is attractive to the country's youth.

Gangsters in Movies

The television and film industry is partly responsible for creating the notion that gang life is exciting and even enviable. For decades, gangs have been a force to be reckoned with on the Big Screen. In 1961, *West Side Story*, a popular Broadway musical about ethnic New York gangs of the 1950s, was made into a movie that earned ten Oscars. A decade later in 1972, the movie *The Godfather*, about the Mafia lifestyle, was released and won three Oscars. *The Godfather* and its two sequels became one of the most famous and popular movie trilogies of all time. Since *The Godfather*, movies about gangs have been numerous and popular. Among them are 1991's *Boyz 'n the Hood*, about inner-city gang life in Los Angeles, which was nominated for two Oscars. Director Martin Scorsese's *Gangs of New York*, a movie about gang life in the 1800s, earned ten Oscar nominations in 2003. In 2001 Denzel Washington won the Best Actor Oscar for his role as a Los Angeles gang cop with controversial methods in *Training Day*. Washington later starred in 2007's *American Gangster*, which received two Oscar nominations. Even TV has had a gang presence, as in the award-winning, Mafia-themed drama series *The Sopranos*. The popularity of the gang theme in American TV and cinema is evidence that Americans are enthralled with the gang lifestyle on screen. Although gang shows are often violent stories of heartbreak and hardship, they also tend to idolize the gang way of life. "In a bizarre way, this glorification of gangster life provides young wannabe gangsters with an acceptable and desirable role to be sought and achieved in American society,"[57] says Yablonsky.

The Godfather glorified and romanticized Mafia gang life. It started a trend of Mafia-related gangster movies.

Gangsters in Music

If movies have had a role in making gang culture popular in the past few decades, the music industry arguably has borne even more responsibility for glorifying gangs. Hip hop music, which originated in the 1960s, quickly rocketed to chart-topping status, and the rap/hip hop genre is one of the most popular kinds of music in America today. It is also the favorite music of gangs. In the 1980s and 1990s, many hip hop stars branched into a new music genre called gangsta rap. They often wrote and performed songs in the first-person as stories about the gang way of life. Many popular gangsta rap songs have had titles and lyrics that make undeniable references to gangs, such as "Why We Thugs" by Ice Cube and "Gangsta's Paradise" by Coolio. Ice Cube and Coolio, like several other gangsta rap stars, were affiliated with gangs before their music became famous.

Former gang member Coolio accepts a Grammy for his song "Gangsta's Paradise" in 1996. Many rap stars were affiliated with gangs before becoming rappers.

Gangsta rap, although very popular, is also controversial. People have protested the music for its bad language and violent lyrics and for promoting brutality against police. Gangsta rap songs and music videos are also notorious for their insulting, sexist portrayals of women. "It's pornographic smut,"[58] said the late C. DeLores Tucker, former head of the National Political Congress of Black Women and an outspoken critic of gangsta rap. The music has been harshly criticized for idolizing gangs and encouraging young people to take part in a lifestyle of crime, murder, and abuse of women. "A gangster is a criminal," said Tucker, and "gangsta rap is criminal activity."[59]

Defenders of gang music, meanwhile, say that the First Amendment to the U.S. Constitution, which guarantees all Americans the right to free speech, allows gangsta rap stars to sing whatever they want. The music's defenders also claim that music alone does not force or even encourage anyone to join a gang or commit gang-related crimes, and that in fact, the majority of this music's audience are not gang members at all. "Gangsta rap's largest population of fans, judging by concert attendance and record sales, has always been white suburban youth,"[60] says Emmett George Price III, a national expert on African American music and culture. The majority of gangs, on the other hand, are made up of inner-city, minority populations, suggesting that gangsta rap is not really a driving force behind gang membership.

Nevertheless, many experts do believe that the widespread popularity of gangsta rap music helps explain why so many young people in America seem to be attracted to the gang lifestyle. Some rap songs imply that there is a link between listening to rap music and participating in gang life, such as Ice Cube's 2008 hit "Gangsta Rap Made Me Do It." In some communities where gang presence is either new or has recently been on the rise, police also say there is a definite connection between the appearance of hip hop clubs that play gangsta music and a rise in street violence. "When you have music that says it's basically O.K. to treat women poorly, to steal things and to confront and shoot police officers, you'll attract a small percentage of the population that wants to lead the thug life,"[61] says Thomas Harris, a police lieutenant in

Murder Rap

By the late 1990s, Tupac Shakur and Biggie Smalls (also known as Notorious B.I.G.) had become two of the country's biggest names in gangsta rap. They were natural rivals, not just in music but in gang ties: Tupac was affiliated with the Bloods and Biggie Smalls with the Crips, two gangs with a long-standing and violent vendetta against each other.

On September 7, 1996, Tupac Shakur was shot multiple times in a car in Las Vegas, Nevada, and later died from his injuries. The police gang unit from his hometown of Compton, California, immediately suspected the murder was gang-related. His death set off a spate of gang violence and murder in Southern California. Eight months after Tupac died, his archrival, Biggie Smalls, was also killed in a drive-by shooting in Los Angeles on May 9, 1997. Even though the murders of two rival gangsta rap stars fueled objections to their music, Tupac and Biggie became martyrs, and their deaths only made their music more popular.

Rapper Tupac Shakur's 1996 gang-related murder sparked a spate of gang violence between the Bloods and the Crips.

Colorado Springs, Colorado. Price admits that "numerous artists have been sued, with claims that their violent lyrics influenced murders and other extremely violent acts."[62]

There is little doubt that music and movies with gang themes glorify gangs and create an interest in the gang culture; however, gangs have been around for hundreds of years—much longer than radio, television, or movie theaters have existed in America. Modern-day media may help create ideas about gangs that capture people's imagination, but the real attraction to the gang lifestyle outdates the media and probably exists much closer to the gang itself. A gang's success depends less on the media's glorification of it than on its own ability to convince potential members that it is desirable to belong to a gang.

Gangs as Local Icons

For the most part, gangs are a local phenomenon. They begin in a particular neighborhood, and with rare exception, they remain in the same place. The idea that music and movies known around the nation encourage young people to start gangs perhaps misses the point that most gangs define themselves not as national but as local groups. Most have a fierce loyalty to their own part of town, even down to the very street they live on. The gang lifestyle may be nationally glorified in songs and films, but very few gang members are out for national fame and glory. They are just trying to make a name for themselves in their own small corner of the world. According to Klein and Maxson, "Gang culture permeated through the popular media (movies, music, clothing styles) seems to have more influence on local gang activity"[63] than it does on a national scale. In other words, nationwide media do not create gangs where there are none; they mainly influence the lifestyle of local gangs that already exist.

The local nature of most street gangs, in fact, defines almost everything about them: their name, their territory or "turf," the hand signals they use to identify themselves, and the gang logos their members tattoo on their bodies or spray paint on walls. Gangs often choose names based on the area of the town or city where they originated: Los Angeles has a gang called 18th Street, for example, while Oklahoma City has the South Side

Locos. Larger gangs often break into smaller branches called sets, and these too can have special loyalty to a certain street or neighborhood, as in the 43rd Street Crips, a set of the larger Crips gang in Los Angeles. Many gangs' symbols or mottoes even include the telephone area code of the place they call home. A gang's loyalty to its own location is a defining feature of most gangs, and this locality may be the gang's main tool for promoting itself and convincing new members to join.

Gang Recruitment

Earning notoriety and admiration within their own neighborhood or part of town is the main way most gangs actually expand. Despite movies and music that might portray the gang lifestyle as heroic or exciting to anyone who watches or listens, those who join gangs do so not because they saw a movie or heard a song but because there is a gang in their neighborhood to join. Most advertising for gangs takes place on the street, by word of mouth. "Members typically advertise membership through distinctive dress, behaviors, or the guarding of territory,"[64] says Englander. Young people who live in a gang's neighborhood are surrounded by constant advertisements of the gang lifestyle, and their nearness to actual gangsters has a much stronger pull on potential members than do gang movies or music. Gang researchers Scott H. Decker and Barrik Van Winkle studied gangs in St. Louis, Missouri, in the early 1990s and discovered that "in every instance, joining the gang was the result of a process that evolved over a period of time. . . . [Members] had grown up in the same neighborhood as other gang members and had done things with them for a lengthy period of time."[65] This suggests that actually growing up around gangs, not just being exposed to gang-related media, is behind most young people's interest in joining a gang. "It ain't just something you come and pick up," says a member of the North Side Mafia gang in Denver, Colorado. "This is something that's put into you from when you're a little kid."[66]

A Web of Gangs

On the other hand, there is evidence that some gangs *have* begun to recruit new members using the media, particularly the Internet.

According to the National Gang Intelligence Center, "Gang members often use cell phones and the Internet to communicate and promote their illicit activities" and to "boast about their gang membership and related activities."[67] Many gangs have a presence on social networking sites such as Facebook and MySpace and the video-sharing site YouTube. Young people who do not yet belong to gangs can easily watch footage that glorifies gang life, chat with gang members on discussion forums, and download the insignias of their favorite gangs. In some communities, police believe the Internet now creates a lot of gang interest among kids, even those as young as eight or ten years old. Some large gangs have their own Web sites that glorify the gang. "It's really no different than the way [Nazi leader Adolf] Hitler recruited Hitler youth with the pageantry and the uniforms and the messages of unity and sacrifice and honor," says Alejandro Vilchez, a youth counselor in Oakland, California. "It's the same messages that you see on these gang websites."[68]

A GANG WILL GROW

"There's a very small window of opportunity when a gang forms when you can destroy it, and if you don't destroy it at birth, it's like a cancer. It will grow, it will spread, and you will never ever get rid of it. You will spend generations fighting it as it evolves and becomes more sophisticated and more complex. In the end, the gang will win."—Yves Lavigne, author of *Hells Angels at War*.

Quoted in "Biker Wars," *Gangland, Season 4*, DVD, produced by Steven Feinartz and Tracy Ullman, A&E Home Video, 2009.

Despite the rise in gang-related Internet sites in recent years, gangs may not have much success in recruiting full-fledged members online. For one thing, gang activity has traditionally been heaviest in low-income neighborhoods where not many families would be expected to have home computers and easy access to the Internet. Even though Internet access is available to most kids and teenagers at places like schools, libraries,

The tattoo parlor Kasper's World has a Web site that has been linked to the 18th Street gang's Web site. Gangs are becoming more Internet savvy.

and community centers, those who access gang information over the Internet may be more gangster wannabes than potential gangsters. "Teens who are having difficulties fitting into a healthy group of friends may seek involvement in a gang . . . and establish sites or engage in discussions that make it appear that they are gang members,"[69] says Nancy E. Willard, director of the Center for Safe and Responsible Internet Use. The Internet's actual success at boosting membership in real gangs, though, is a matter of debate. "The gangs we deal with build their relationships on loyalty, trust and friendship," says Chuck Zeglin, a Los Angeles Police Department gang expert, "and there's no way of getting that on the Internet."[70]

News Media and the Gang Image

For gangs that face a constant barrage of threats from rivals, a tough image is everything, and their "don't mess with us" attitude is something they advertise in every way they can. Surprisingly, the news media, more than any other media venue, may do the most to help gangs spread this message. With every evening news spot and every newspaper article that discusses gang violence, gangs seem more brutal. In harsh inner-city environments, where self-protection is part of life, the media's portrayal of gangs as violent defenders of their own members and turf may send a message to those living in gang neighborhoods that gangs should be left alone and that everyone, even the police, should fear them. By constantly showing the dangers of gangs, the media may unintentionally send the message that the only way to keep from being a victim of gang violence is to join a gang for protection, which is a leading reason many gang members actually do say they joined. "If you're in a hostile environment, and you don't have a family, you're out there fighting by yourself,"[71] says a member of Aryan Circle, a mostly white prison and street gang that originated in Texas in the 1980s.

Both news media and gangs themselves might be achieving the very same goals by touting gangs as widespread violent menaces, but some gang researchers say the overall gang reputation is exaggerated. "Two sources in particular have a tendency to misrepresent the characteristics and activities of youth gangs: the gangs themselves and the media," says Howell. "These are common sources of popular images of youth gangs in the United States. However, most youth gangs are not as formidable as these sources would have us believe."[72] It could be that the news media, in an effort to keep their audience's attention, make gangs out to be enormous and violent problems. And gangs, whose self-preservation depends on making their enemies believe they are vicious and ruthless, only benefit from the negative media attention.

From Wannabe to Member

Whatever forces really drive young people to join gangs—be they movies or music, Web sites or news stories, or circumstances in one's own neighborhood—the attraction of gang life must be overwhelmingly strong, because getting into a gang is neither painless nor easy. Members must go to great lengths to prove themselves worthy. Most gangs require potential members to take part in a jump-in, a ritual in which the recruit must fight a group of several gang members for a certain amount of time. Those who do not surrender or back down during this fierce beating earn the gang's acceptance. Those who fail to impress the gang at a jump-in, on the other hand, are excluded from membership, and some gangs, such as Mara Salvatrucha 13, have even been known to kill wannabe members who show weakness during a jump-in.

Out of Control

"We've lost control of our members, and now we have a monster on our hands."—K.D., female member of the Aryan Circle gang.

Quoted in "Aryan Terror," *Gangland, Season 4*, DVD, produced by Steven Feinartz and Tracy Ullman, A&E Home Video, 2009.

Aside from the jump-in, many gangs also require potential members to commit a serious crime for the gang, ranging from robbery to murder. And for female members, the initiation process often includes forcing a recruit into a "gang rape," during which she must have sex with multiple gang members before being admitted into the gang. In some gangs, the initiation process for female members involves sexual intercourse with a gang member who is known to be infected with the human immunodeficiency virus (HIV), an incurable and fatal illness that is transmitted during unprotected sex. Only girls who would agree to do this are judged to be willing to die for the gang, which is ultimately the expectation most gangs have of their members.

'Til Death Do You Part

Once a person is admitted into a gang, the group demands nothing less than the willingness to sacrifice his or her life for it. "Conventional wisdom portrays gang membership as a lifetime affiliation," say Klein and Maxson. "Once you're a crip, you're a crip for life."[73] Gang members readily subscribe to this idea from the moment they become part of a gang. Lifelong loyalty to the gang is considered the most important gang philosophy, and in almost any gang in America, the number one rule is that gang "brothers" do not snitch on one another—come what may, a gang member will never give police information that could send another gang member to prison. Though the gangs of America are widely diverse, these two demands—self-sacrifice and the expectation of lifelong loyalty—are common to almost all of them. But gangs are like a trap. Murders and arrest rates among gang members soar, and all the while, gangs sell their "gang for life" ideology to members in order to keep them from fleeing. "The viability of their gang depends on the ability of gang members to maintain the perception that leaving the gang is nearly impossible,"[74] say Decker and criminologist Janet L. Lauritsen. Successful gangs do this very convincingly. Jon Hagedorn calls

Deadly Dress Codes

Gangs are territorial and often have violent rivalries with other gangs. To differentiate their members from their enemies, most gangs adopt a dress code or street uniform. For example, Crips and Sureños prefer dark blue clothing such as shirts, ball caps, and bandanas. Bloods, who are rivals to Crips, and Nortenos, who are rivals to Surenos, tend to identify with red. Gang membership is shown in other ways, too, such as the way members wear their clothes. Some wear belts with the buckles off-center to the left or right, for example, and some wear pants with one leg rolled up. Some gangs claim a particular sports team's colors and logo as their symbols.

Gangs often challenge each other for no other reason than clothing. Wearing what appears to be a rival gang's "uniform"—a blue or red shirt, for example—in the wrong part of town can be considered a challenge, whether the offender is a gang member or not. In 2009 a Hispanic college student was shot and killed by gangsters in Daly City, California, only because his companions (none of them gang members) were wearing red. Such tragedies demonstrate the dangers gangs pose even to people who are not in them.

Law enforcement officials say that despite an honor code of not snitching, gang members often are ready to talk to stay out of prison.

gangs "living organisms, instilling in their members, as well as the community, a belief in the organization itself."[75]

The believability of a gang as a tight and unbreakable group does not always hold up when the gang is under pressure, however. "The age distribution of gang members and virtually every study of gangs belies this conventional wisdom"[76] that gang membership is really for life, say Klein and Maxson. Gangs consist mostly of teenagers and young adults, suggesting that at some point in adulthood, a majority of gang members decide to leave the gang—it is not really a commitment most members continue forever. And when their gang activity gets them in trouble with the law, a great many gang members are also quick to break the no-snitching rule the gang expects them to uphold. "They'll tell you morning, noon, and night that 'these are my brothers, these are my associates, and we're in this blood in and blood out' kind of thing," says Tim Twining, chief deputy district attorney in Denver, Colorado. The reality, he says, is that snitching is common. "When the chips really fall on the table, and it's 'you're going to prison for the rest of your life or you tell the truth,' we'll often get the truth."[77]

Gangs may do a great job of creating or sustaining a heroic image of themselves, using everything at their disposal, from movies and music to the Internet and street-level recruiting, to make their lifestyle seem thrilling and enviable. They depict themselves as family-like associations with lifelong, unbreakable bonds. And it may be these characteristics that draw so many young people into the gang lifestyle despite the torture many must endure to get into the gang and the horrifying violence to which they are exposed once they are members. The reality of most gangs, however, is that the very philosophies around which they build their membership, such as brotherhood for life and putting the gang before everything else, might be mere myths that gangs do a good job of keeping alive. Gang membership is not glorious. At their heart, most gangs are really about death, prison, and betrayal. It is up to communities to find a better way to teach this lesson to young people before they join gangs. This may be the only hope for a solution to America's problems with gangs.

GANGS AND SOCIETY

Gang presence and membership has been on the rise almost everywhere in recent decades, not just in the crowded cities where gangs traditionally have existed but in smaller cities, suburbs of cities, and even rural areas. According to the National Gang Center, there was a 33 percent rise from 2002 to 2007 in the number of suburban police jurisdictions that reported gang problems, and a 25 percent rise in gang problems reported in rural counties. In big cities during the same period, the percentage of reported gang problems rose 12 percent, about one-half to one-third the increase in rural areas and suburbs. Clearly, gangs are not just an inner-city problem. They appeal to kids, teens, and young adults in a variety of areas and for a variety of reasons. Lack of adult supervision during childhood, living in poverty with few or no good job options, the ability to make big money by committing crimes, schools that do a poor job of making students feel important, and dangerous neighborhoods where young people fear for their own safety have all been blamed for the appearance and growth of gangs across the country. Each of these factors likely contributes to gang membership in some way, and they are things that communities may be able to do something about. But people tend to think of gangs as an issue of crime, not of society, and if gang violence flares up in a community, police are usually expected to deal with it or are blamed if gang violence gets out of hand. Many communities are said to ignore their growing gang population completely, even to deny it, until a violent gang incident erupts that makes them take notice. According to the National Gang Center, "Local officials may be reluctant to acknowledge their gang problem until it publicly surfaces in a tragic event, or they may declare they have successfully dealt with it, only to see it surface again."[78]

The presence of gangs is often understated or treated like a taboo, so gang activity takes a community by surprise when it surges into the public sphere. Stories of gang-related violence and murder hit the news and people respond to the tragedy with outrage. Innocent bystanders sometimes get hit by stray bullets if gang members start shooting at each other in public places. Such incidents happen more often as gangs crop up in more communities and become more violent. Some gang researchers say that rarely do gangs really intend to hurt or kill innocent people. In fact, says gang researcher Donnie Harris, the opposite may be the case. "For the most part gang members have codes they live by which include not hurting children" or "old or religious people,"[79] he says. Nevertheless, gang violence often erupts blindly and endangers not just gang members but anyone else who happens to be nearby, and when this occurs, the community, city, state, and nation express shock and concern about the growing problem of gangs.

WASTED CHANCES

"Young people who join gangs have made a choice to squander the opportunities that await in life, and their choices put the lives of innocent Americans in danger."—U.S. senator Orrin Hatch of Utah.

Quoted in "Senate Unanimously Passes Feinstein-Hatch Comprehensive Gang Legislation," press release from Senator Hatch's office, September 21, 2007. http://hatch.senate.gov/public/index.cfm?FuseAction=PressReleases.View&PressRelease_id=a974015b-884d-4b20-9ff1-69a4f0f6e49f.

It is important for cities, towns, and communities to realize that the gang "problem" that leads to tragic shootings and other violence does not appear overnight. By the time gang-related violence and crime have erupted in a community, gangs usually have been present long enough for at least two different groups to establish themselves, recruit members, obtain weapons, and

Community officials are often reluctant to acknowledge their gang problem until a tragic shooting sparks community dismay and outrage.

develop a rivalry that leads to violent public clashes. Publicly confirming that gangs exist in a community is something that should happen much earlier than it does. "Failure to recognize or acknowledge the existence of gang activity . . . dramatically increases a gang's ability to thrive and develop a power base," say criminal justice experts Kären Hess and Christine Orthmann. Yet, among the communities they have studied, they say several "began to address gang issues only when high-profile gang-related incidents occurred."[80] By the time many communities are ready to admit to a gang problem, gangs may be deeply rooted, and a gang-related tragedy has probably happened already. But the victims of gangs are not just innocent people caught in the cross fire of a gang shooting or people who live in or near gang-related parts of cities and towns. Gangs affect everyone, and everyone shares in the responsibility of reducing the negative impacts gangs have on society.

Everyone Is a Victim

The cost to the public of gangs is enormous. In neighborhoods where gangs are deeply entrenched, gang activity keeps citizens and businesses in a constantly watchful state. Businesses fear becoming victims of gang-related robberies or crime. Even if gang members just like to shop or eat at local stores or restaurants, other customers may then stay away, so the venues lose business. In gang-ridden neighborhoods, parents worry that it is unsafe for their kids to walk to and from school, because gang-related shootings could happen anywhere at any time. Community parks where people would normally take walks or have picnics and where kids would normally play are often taken over by gangs as places to sell drugs, and they become dangerous sites of gang violence that the rest of the community completely avoids. Fear of gang violence keeps people indoors, especially at night when gang members are out in full force. Neighborhoods that gangs call home become such terrible places for anyone else to live or do business that law-abiding people tend to move out of these neighborhoods if they can, leaving behind an almost entirely criminal population.

Gang-infested neighborhoods quickly become blights on their cities.

Journalist Tony Rizzo describes a gang-infested area of Kansas City, Missouri, this way: "On nearly every block, well-kept homes sit next to trashed and ruined houses stripped by thieves and enveloped by saplings and head-high weeds. Abandoned tires dot the streets. Huge piles of household furnishings rot on curbs, left by evictees unable to pay rent to absentee landlords. Bullet perforations in houses are as common as feral cats and unleashed dogs."[81] Gang neighborhoods quickly become a blight on a city, and citizens often cannot keep up with the costs of keeping the community clean and safe.

Why Gangs Cost Money

Ugly, run-down gang neighborhoods that take away from a community's appearance and productivity are not the only financial cost of gangs to the public. Police departments that form gang units to deal specifically with gang-related crime are funded with tax dollars, so the more a police department has to deal with gang issues, the more expensive it is to run. Police departments flooded with responses to gang crime have less time and resources to deal with issues like traffic patrol, nongang crime, and general public safety. The cost of controlling gang violence and crime is a heavy burden on communities and depletes public funds that otherwise could be spent on things like schools, parks, and recreation programs. People who do not live in or near a city's gang neighborhoods and are rarely affected by gangs still see their tax dollars going toward the problem, and some of them question whether that is fair. Since even a strong police gang unit cannot protect a community from all gang crime, many people also question just how well their tax money is being spent for gang prevention. For example, a 2009 editorial in the *Los Angeles Times* claimed that the city of Los Angeles has "floundered with anti-gang efforts for years, throwing money at programs without knowing whether they were working or even defining what they were supposed to accomplish."[82]

While it is true that police forces more specialized at dealing with gang problems usually *do* have a greater rate of success at getting gang members off the streets, sending gang members to prison costs taxpayers, too. Prisons are swelling with an ever-increasing population of gangsters. In some areas, a majority of the growing prison population now consists of gang members. It seems as though gangsters are merely being transferred from streets to prisons, where the cost of housing them and feeding them is a growing burden on taxpayers. All the while, inside prison, the gang culture is alive and well. "You can't arrest your way out of gang type situations,"[83] says Paul Joyce, a former police superintendent in Boston, Massachusetts.

The cost of gangs extends far beyond neighborhood crime and taxpayer-funded policing and imprisonment. Gangs create a social deficit as well. Kids and teens who are drawn toward gang life are pulled into a dead-end future. Many gang members are high school dropouts, become teenage parents, and start building a criminal record at a young age, things that will only make it more difficult for them to break away from the gang lifestyle to pursue an education, a career, and a rewarding future. Few gang members have regular jobs or pay a share of the taxes needed to address the problems their gang creates. Gangs contribute little to the betterment of society, but they attract many young people to a life of crime, individuals whose intelligence and talents may never reach their full potential because of their gang membership. "It has been estimated that at least 25% of adolescents in America are at serious risk of not achieving productive adulthood,"[84] says Harris. Gangs are not the only reason these youths are at risk, but gang membership does have a negative outcome for many if not most gang members. Destroying young people's potential may be how gangs cost society the most.

We Are All Responsible

America's widespread gang presence affects everyone in some way, and there are no easy answers for how the spread of criminal gang activity can be quelled. Just the same, there are things society can do to address gang-related problems. Gangs are often branded as a violent, costly, and unwanted criminal plague. Yet, not all gang members are criminals, and not all criminals belong to gangs. "Law enforcement officers must maintain objectivity and refrain from stereotyping gang members,"[85] say Hess and Orthmann.

Members of the Salinas, California, police gang suppression unit enter a home of known gang members as part of a major crackdown on gangs on California's Central Coast.

Stereotyping likely only reinforces gangsters' instincts to stick together and oppose police. Society should also remember that the growth of gangs is a symptom of other social issues. Focusing only on putting gang members in jail is not a long-term answer for dealing with gangs. Society instead must concentrate on what makes people join gangs and stay in them, then give potential and current gang members different, more positive ways to meet the needs that gangs fulfill. Gang researchers have come up with a three-part strategy for accomplishing this, and it has been successful at cutting back on gang membership and activity in many communities.

The first part of the strategy is called suppression, and it includes methods for responding to existing gang problems and cutting back on gang crime. Largely a police effort, suppression tactics include an increase in surveillance of gang hangouts and the targeted gang sweeps that result in arrests of a gang's most active criminal members. Suppression tactics often result in a rapid cutback of gang activity and an almost immediate, if temporary, drop in the crime rate of gang-infested neighborhoods. Suppression is often so successful at bringing about rapid improvements that communities mistakenly think their gang problem has been solved. Often, though, suppression just forces gangs to regroup and to rebuild their strength. "The use of singular suppression tactics in combating gangs and gun crime still has a mixed report card," says Howell. "Calls are often made for better implementation of problem-oriented or problem-solving policing."[86] In the period of quiet that often occurs after a gang sweep or other suppression tactic, research suggests that police and communities both need to focus on a second strategy: intervention.

Not all gang members are equally committed to their gang or to the gang lifestyle. In fact, following a period of police suppression, most of a gang's most criminal-minded members may be in jail, and this gives police and community activists a chance to intervene or work with remaining gang members to try to persuade them away from the pull of the gang. Intervention focuses on giving active gang members opportunities to break away from the gang lifestyle by helping them complete or further their education, get jobs, find a place to live that is away from their former gang neighborhood, and even remove gang tattoos that mark a gang member as an enemy to other gangs and as a criminal to potential employers.

Intervention, like suppression, has had a lot of success in communities. In Las Vegas, Nevada, for example, an intervention program called Back on Track has helped thousands of gang members in the city leave their gang, go back to school, and get jobs. "We get to see kids from the projects maturing and building skill sets," says Melvin Ennis, the program's administrator. He estimates that the intervention tactics have an 80 percent success rate in turning young people away from Las Vegas gangs. "We got kids in college,"[87] he says. However, intervention is a response to an already established gang population. Many researchers say that the third part of the gang strategy, prevention, is the most important, because if it is successful, it may keep gangs from forming at all.

Prevention is probably the area in which society as a whole can take the most responsibility for its gang issues. Prevention targets various social problems that are believed to lead to gang membership—things like a lack of safe places for kids to hang out and play in their communities, or schools that make little effort to engage students in active learning and steer them toward exciting and positive careers. Since child abuse and neglect are considered factors that put young people at risk of joining gangs, communities also may be able to improve family relationships by educating parents and providing more resources, like child care, for working parents. "Children do not choose the families into which they are born, the communities where they live, the schools they attend," says Howell. Reducing risks of gang participation, he says, "involves changing conditions to which youth are exposed that negatively affect their life chances."[88]

THE OTHER 90 PERCENT

"The biggest cause of gangs is we do nothing for the 90 percent who aren't gang members. If all the attention and respect goes to the gang members, then what happens to the kids who aren't getting that attention and are getting beaten up by gang members?"— Richard Valdemar, retired Los Angeles gang investigator.

Quoted in Melanie Basich, "TREXPO West: Are Gang Members Hopeless?" *Police: The Law Enforcement Magazine*, May 1, 2009.

Prevention strategies alone are not likely to eliminate the gang problem, at least not overnight, and communities are sometimes criticized for spending public money in an attempt to fix people's private financial and home-life problems. Still, gang prevention measures, combined with intervention and suppression, are widely considered the best ways for society to address the growing gang problem, as shown by recent successes in several major cities. In Los Angeles County, California, this three-part strategy was given credit for reducing gang-related crime by up to 20 percent in early 2010. And in Richmond, Virginia, the Gang Reduction Intervention Program, which also uses the three-part gang strategy, has won national awards for success at reducing gang activity. Across the country, communities are trying similar strategies for dealing with gangs

Investment in Hope

Communities around the country are giving opportunities to local gang members to help them turn their lives around. One example is Bradenton, Florida, home to as many as twenty different gangs, where a business called Honeycomb Company of America regularly hires gang members into manufacturing jobs. A legal job is an important first step to breaking ties with gang life. In fact, gangs often threaten their members with violence to discourage them from looking for jobs in the nongang world, since finding employment usually leads to leaving a gang. "We know how hard the pressure they get is on the street not to take part in being a productive worker in society," says Honeycomb president Daniel Judge Jr., who hired twelve gang members between 2007 and 2010. The fact that companies like Honeycomb are willing to take a chance on gang members, and in return are finding gang members willing to take a chance on nongang life, is a good sign that communities can do something to change the trend of gang growth, violence, and hopelessness.

Quoted in Robert Napper, "Local Company's Anti-gang Efforts Net Award," *Bradenton Herald*, March 25, 2010. www.bradenton.com/2010/03/25/2156869/local-companys-anti-gang-efforts.html.

and are receiving encouraging results.

Dispelling Gang Myths

Perhaps the most vital thing society can do to diminish gang-related problems is to educate all people, gang members or not, about the realities of gang life. Too many people have misconceptions about gangs, and these only serve to worsen gang problems. Gangs tend to foster these misconceptions and strive to keep them going, but if more people were aware of certain facts about gangs, such as the rate at which gang members are injured, killed, or sent to prison, fewer people might be inclined to join a gang, and society might be more successful at keeping young people from being interested in gangs in the first place.

One widespread myth about gangs is that they are all about loyalty and a sense of family. In reality, fear, not loyalty, holds most gangs together. Many gang members say they joined a gang primarily out of fear; it had become too dangerous in their gang-ridden neighborhood not to belong to a gang. Contrary to what many people believe, researchers have found that most gangs do not recruit members through direct threats or violence; they instead recruit by offering protection from other violent gangs. According to the National Gang Center, "Few youth, irrespective of race/ethnicity, report they have been forced or coerced to join a gang."[89] But once they are in a gang, most members who remain do so because they fear retaliation from the gang if they were to leave, and they also fear the unknown world outside the gang. Poorly educated, with no guarantee that they could find a job or a place to live, many members stay in the gang because it is the only lifestyle they know. "Factors that make leaving a gang more difficult include greater dependence on or personal status in the group, continuing perceptions by others (e.g., rivals) that the person is a bona fide member of the gang, and the lack of viable lifestyle alternatives," says the National Gang Center. According to research studies, however, gang members who wanted out "typically left a gang without complication or facing any serious

Signs of Wanting to Be a Gangster

Prevention tactics aimed at reducing gang-related problems in America focus on educating kids and teens at risk of becoming gang members about alternatives to gang life. Those at risk of joining gangs often show certain warning signs, including the following:

Dressing in a particular gang's colors

Drawing gang graffiti

Learning and using a gang's hand signals

Listening to gang music

Spending time at known gang hangouts

Associating with gang members

Developing behavior problems at home or school

consequences"[90] from the gang itself. So an important part of gang intervention strategies may be informing gang members that it *is* possible to safely leave a gang and that alternatives and support systems do exist.

Another common misconception about gangs is that they are profitable and that by selling drugs and committing other kinds of crimes for money, gang members become wealthy. In reality, most gangs are formed in poor communities, and the majority of their members continue to dwell in poverty. "Despite enormous risks to health, life, and freedom" as a result of working for a gang, says Siegel, "average gang members earned only slightly more than what they could earn in the legitimate labor market (about $6 to $11 per hour)."[91] The few who do make a good living from their criminal gang activity are unfortunately more likely to be targets of violence from rival gangs or even rival members of their own gang, especially if their successful criminal business cuts into someone else's profits. They may also draw police attention to themselves or to the gang. In the end, says Siegel, "the gang boys' greed causes them to overestimate the potential for future criminal gain versus the probability of apprehension and punishment."[92]

Gangs Are Dead-Ends

Beneath all the myths, an important reality of gangs is that they typically lead to one of two outcomes: going to prison for gang-related crime and murder or becoming a victim of gang-related crime or murder. Society must become more successful at spreading word of this gang reality and providing good alternative ways for young people to avoid it if the problem of criminal gangs is ever to disappear. Society, too, must learn to see gangs not as a scourge but as an institution that for centuries has met the needs of certain people when society has failed them. Most gangs are signs of social problems and a result of social strife. As hard as it may be to address gang problems, gangs themselves are an increasingly powerful force in society, one that cannot be ignored. Vigil calls the gang phenomenon a subsociety, an offshoot from the rest of the community that arises when a certain group feels left out of mainstream culture. "Once this

Beneath the myths of gang life lies the reality of a probable end in either jail or death.

subsociety has been created to meet the needs of its creators," he says, "it persists and becomes an urban fixture in certain neighborhoods, compelling future generations of youth to join it or otherwise come to terms with it."[93] Coming to terms with gangs is one of the ongoing social challenges of the times.

NOTES

Chapter 1: The History of Gangs in America

1. "In the Spotlight: Gangs," National Criminal Justice Reference Service, September 23, 2009. www.ncjrs.gov/spotlight/gangs/summary.html.
2. David Kale, *The Boston Harbor Islands: A History of an Urban Wilderness*. Charleston, SC: History Press, 2007, p. 67.
3. Larry J. Siegel, *Introduction to Criminal Justice*. Belmont, CA: Wadsworth, 2009, p. 5.
4. Thomas Reppetto, *American Mafia: A History of Its Rise to Power*. New York: Henry Holt, 2004, p. 21.
5. Steven David Valdivia, *Forces . . . Gangs to Riots: Why and How Some Communities Erupt and How We May End It*. Raleigh, NC: LULU, p. 11.
6. Reppetto, *American Mafia*, p. 21.
7. Reppetto, *American Mafia*, p. 22.
8. Reppetto, *American Mafia*, p. 18.
9. Donald J. Shoemaker, *Juvenile Delinquency*. Lanham, MD: Rowman & Littlefield, 2009, p. 260.
10. Quoted in Lee Daniels, "House of UMOJA," *Black Enterprise*, May 1981, p. 30.

Chapter 2: Gangs and Culture

11. Xue Lan Rong and Judith Preissle, *Educating Immigrant Students in the 21st Century: What Educators Need to Know*, 2nd ed. Thousand Oaks, CA: Corwin Press, 2009, p. 45.
12. Malcolm W. Klein and Cheryl L. Maxson, *Street Gang Patterns and Policies*. New York: Oxford University Press, 2006, pp. 207–8.
13. Angelo N. Ancheta, *Race, Rights, and the Asian American Experience*, 2nd ed. New Brunswick, NJ: Rutgers University Press, 2006, p. 11.

14. Robert M. Regoli, John D. Hewitt, and Matt DeLisi, *Deliquency in Society*, 8th ed. Sudbury, MA: Jones and Bartlett, 2010, p. 512.
15. Catherine H. Conly, *Street Gangs: Current Knowledge and Strategies*. Darby, PA: Diane, 1993, p. 16.
16. James Diego Vigil, *A Rainbow of Gangs: Street Cultures in the Mega-City*. Austin: University of Texas Press, 2003, p. 5.
17. Kären M. Hess, *Introduction to Law Enforcement and Criminal Justice*, 9th ed. Belmont, CA: Wadsworth, 2010, p. 317.
18. Hess, *Introduction to Law Enforcement*, p. 317.
19. Stanley Tookie Williams, *Blue Rage, Black Redemption: A Memoir*. New York: Touchstone, 2004, p. 14.
20. Vigil, *Rainbow of Gangs*, p. 10.
21. Lewis Yablonsky, *Gangsters: 50 Years of Madness, Drugs, and Death on the Streets of America*. New York: New York University Press, 1997, p. 7.
22. Jody Miller, "The Girls in the Gang: What We've Learned from Two Decades of Research," in *Gangs in America III*, edited by C. Ronald Huff. Thousand Oaks, CA: Sage, 2002, p. 177.
23. Kären M. Hess, *Juvenile Justice*, 5th ed. Belmont, CA: Wadsworth, 2004, p. 204.
24. Marc Lacey, "Abuse Trails Central American Girls into Gangs," *New York Times*, April 11, 2008. www.nytimes.com/2008/04/11/world/americas/11guatemala.html?_r=1.
25. Miller, "Girls in the Gang," p. 178.
26. James F. Short, *Poverty, Ethnicity, and Violent Crime*. Boulder, CO: Westview, 1997, p. 102.
27. Vigil, *Rainbow of Gangs*, p. 7.

Chapter 3: Gangs as Businesses

28. Ian Bannon and Maria C. Corriea, introduction to *The Other Half of Gender: Men's Issues in Development*, edited by Ian Bannon and Maria C. Corriea. Washington, DC: World Bank, 2006, p. xxii.
29. Larry J. Siegel, *Criminology*, 10th ed. Belmont, CA: Thomson Higher Education, 2009, p. 107.
30. James C. Howell, "The Impact of Gangs on Communities," *NYGC Bulletin*, August 2006, p. 3.

31. Donnie Harris, *Gangland: The Growing Gang Epidemic in America's Cities.* Oak Ridge, TN: Holy Fire, 2004, p. 41.
32. Deborah Lamm Weisel, *Contemporary Gangs: An Organizational Analysis.* El Paso, TX: LBF Scholarly Publishing, 2004, p. 38.
33. Anne Turnbaugh Lockwood, *Conversations with Educational Leaders: Contemporary Viewpoints on Education.* Albany: State University of New York Press, 1997, p. 45.
34. Thomas A. Reppetto, *Bringing Down the Mob: The War Against the American Mafia.* New York: Henry Holt, 2006, p. 234.
35. Martín Sánchez Jankowski, *Islands in the Street: Gangs and American Urban Society.* Berkeley and Los Angeles: University of California Press, 1991, p. 70.
36. Jankowski, *Islands in the Street*, p. 91.
37. Felix M. Padilla, *The Gang as an American Enterprise.* New Brunswick, NJ: Rutgers University Press, 1992, p. 137.
38. Carmen Gentile, "The Gangs of El Salvador: A Growing Industry," *Time*, September 6, 2009. www.time.com/time/world/article/0,8599,1920741,00.html.
39. Weisel, *Contemporary Gangs*, p. 127.
40. James C. Howell, "Menacing or Mimicking? Realities of Youth Gangs," *Juvenile and Family Court Journal*, Spring 2007, p. 41.
41. Howell, "Menacing or Mimicking?" p. 39.
42. Chris Mathers, *Crime School: Money Laundering; True Crime Meets the World of Business and Finance.* Buffalo, NY: Firefly Books, 2004, p. 42.
43. Siegel, *Juvenile Delinquency*, pp. 294, 300.
44. John Hagedorn, *A World of Gangs: Armed Young Men and Gangsta Culture.* Minneapolis: University of Minnesota Press, 2008, p. 6.
45. Hagedorn, *A World of Gangs*, p. 6.

Chapter 4: Gangs and the Legal System

46. Yablonsky, *Gangsters*, p. 5.
47. Yablonsky, *Gangsters*, p. 5.
48. Elizabeth Kandel Englander, *Understanding Violence*, 3rd ed. Mahwah, NJ: Lawrence Erlbaum, 2007, p. 145.

49. Criminal Intelligence Service Canada (CISC), "Feature Focus: The Illegal Firearms Market in Canada," in *2007 Annual Report on Organized Crime in Canada*. Ottawa: CISC, 2007. www.cisc.gc.ca/annual_reports/annual_report_2007/feature_focus_2007_e.html.

50. Criminal Intelligence Service Canada, "Feature Focus."

51. Criminal Intelligence Service Canada, "Feature Focus."

52. Kody Scott, *Monster: The Autobiography of an L.A. Gang Member*. New York: Grove/Atlantic, 1993, pp. 177-78.

53. Edward Burns, "Gang- and Drug-Related Homicide: Baltimore's Successful Enforcement Strategy," *Bureau of Justice Assistance Bulletin*, July 2003. www.ncjrs.gov/html/bja/gang/pfv.html.

54. Quoted in Pat Pheifer, "St. Paul Teenager Gets 30 Years for Killing Rival Gang Member," *Minneapolis Star Tribune*, January 19, 2010. www.startribune.com/local/stpaul/82127737.html.

55. National Gang Intelligence Center, *National Gang Threat Assessment 2005*. Washington, DC: U.S. Department of Justice, 2005. www.ojp.usdoj.gov/BJA/what/2005_threat_assesment.pdf.

56. Quoted in "Deadly Blast," *Gangland, Season 4*, DVD, produced by Steven Feinartz and Tracy Ullman, A&E Home Video, 2009.

Chapter 5: Promoting Gang Life

57. Yablonsky, *Gangsters*, p. 26.

58. Quoted in Kevin Powell, "Mama Said Knock Out," *Vibe*, September 1995, p. 93.

59. Quoted in Powell, "Mama Said Knock Out," p. 93.

60. Emmett George Price III, *Hip Hop Culture*. Santa Barbara, CA: ABC-CLIO, 2006, p. 59.

61. Quoted in Dan Frosch, "Colorado Police Link Rise in Violence to Music," *New York Times*, September 3, 2007. www.nytimes.com/2007/09/03/us/03hiphop.html.

62. Price, *Hip Hop Culture*, p. 61.

63. Klein and Maxson, *Street Gang Patterns*, p. 57.

64. Englander, *Understanding Violence*, p. 144.

65. Scott H. Decker and Barrik Van Winkle, *Life in the Gang: Family, Friends, and Violence*. New York: Cambridge University Press, 1996, pp. 64-65.

66. Quoted in "Mile High Killers," *Gangland, Season 4*, DVD, produced by Steven Feinartz and Tracy Ullman, A&E Home Video, 2009.

67. National Gang Intelligence Center, *National Gang Threat Assessment 2009*, Washington, DC: U.S. Department of Justice, 2009. www.justice.gov/ndic/pubs32/32146/index.htm#Contents.

68. Quoted in Joe Vazquez, "Gangs Turn to Social Networking Sites to Recruit," CBS-5 Crime Watch, City of Oakland, California, February 7, 2008. http://cbs5.com/local/Internet.gang.recruiting.2.648038.html.

69. Nancy E. Willard, *Cyberbullying and Cyberthreats: Responding to the Challenge of Online Social Aggression, Threats, and Distress*. Champaign, IL: Research Press, 2007, p. 66.

70. Quoted in Carrie Kirby, "Gangs.com: Crews Show Off Their Colors and Lifestyles on Web," *San Francisco Chronicle*, January 6, 2001.

71. Quoted in "Aryan Terror," *Gangland, Season 4*, DVD, produced by Steven Feinartz and Tracy Ullman, A&E Home Video, 2009.

72. Howell, "Menacing or Mimicking?" p. 39.

73. Klein and Maxson, *Street Gang Patterns*, p. 153.

74. Scott H. Decker and Janet L. Lauritsen, "Leaving the Gang," in *Gangs in America*, 3rd ed., edited by C. Ronald Huff. Thousand Oaks, CA: Sage, 2002, p. 61.

75. Hagedorn, *A World of Gangs*, p. 9.

76. Klein and Maxson, *Street Gang Patterns*, p. 153.

77. Quoted in "Mile High Killers," *Gangland, Season 4*, DVD, produced by Steven Feinartz and Tracy Ullman, A&E Home Video, 2009.

Chapter 6: Gangs and Society

78. National Gang Center, "Frequently Asked Questions About Gangs." www.nationalgangcenter.gov/About/FAQ.

79. Harris, *Gangland*, p. 26.

80. Kären M. Hess and Christine Hess Orthmann, *Criminal Investigation*, 9th ed., Clifton Park, NY: Delmar, 2010, p. 590.

81. Tony Rizzo, "Murder Factory, Part 2: Decades of Blight Leave ZIP code 64130 Reeling in Violence," *Kansas City (MO) Star*, January 25, 2009. www.kansascity.com/2009/01/25/1000674/murder-factory-part-2-decades.html.

82. "Should the Times Back a Second Anti-gang Parcel Tax Effort?" Opinion L.A., *Los Angeles Times*, July 8, 2009. http://opinion.latimes.com/opinionla/2009/07/parcel-tax-gang-reduction-los-angeles.html.

83. Quoted in Madison Grey, "How to Turn Around a Gang Member," *Time*, September 2, 2009. www.time.com/time/nation/article/0,8599,1919253,00.html#ixzz0jOyAoP6q.

84. James C. Howell, *Preventing and Reducing Juvenile Delinquency: A Comprehensive Framework*, 2nd ed. Thousand Oaks, CA: Sage, 2009, p. 60.

85. Hess and Orthmann, *Criminal Investigation*, p. 590.

86. Howell, *Reducing Juvenile Delinquency*, p. 156.

87. Quoted in Lynette Curtis, "Back on Track: Clark County's Gang Intervention Team Helps Get Youth off Streets," by *Las Vegas Review Journal*, June 29, 2009. www.lvrj.com/news/49421522.html.

88. Howell, *Reducing Juvenile Delinquency*, p. 60.

89. National Gang Center, "Frequently Asked Questions."

90. National Gang Center, "Frequently Asked Questions."

91. Siegel, *Criminology*, p. 107.

92. Siegel, *Criminology*, 107.

93. Vigil, *A Rainbow of Gangs*, p. 12.

DISCUSSION QUESTIONS

Chapter 1: The History of Gangs in America

1. What does the author mean by "forces" that drive gangs together? What kinds of issues in society might lead to the formation of gangs, and why?
2. What is the relationship between gangs and orphans? What does Thomas Reppetto mean when he says "young men far from home were good candidates for trouble"?
3. How have gangs changed through different periods of U.S. history? What are some things almost all gangs have had in common?

Chapter 2: Gangs and Culture

1. What reasons does the author give for why immigration alone does not create gangs?
2. How are gangs considered different than other social groups that have names, uniforms, logos, and similar identifying features? Is it fair for gangs to be singled out as problem groups? Why or why not?
3. What are some arguments in favor of the idea that gangs serve as families for their members? What are some ways gangs do *not* meet the needs that traditional families do?

Chapter 3: Gangs as Businesses

1. Ian Bannon and Maria C. Corriea say that "education does not provide the same financial rewards for lower-income youth as it does for youth in middle-income groups." Do you agree with this statement? Why or why not?
2. What are some ways that moneymaking gangs resemble society's legal businesses?

3. What does the author mean when she calls gangs a "counter-culture"?

Chapter 4: Gangs and the Legal System

1. The author says that many gang members refer to themselves and their gang in military terms. Why do you think enlisting in the national military is considered acceptable or honorable in American society, while enlisting in a military-like gang is not?
2. If the United States were to monitor its borders more heavily, what effect do you think it would have on the country's gang problems?
3. Why are police sweeps and gang arrests considered a temporary solution to the gang problem?

Chapter 5: Promoting Gang Life

1. C. DeLores Tucker said that gangsta rap music is "criminal activity." What do you think she meant? Do you agree? Why or why not?
2. How do you think kids and teens in the United States have been affected by gang movies and music?
3. What restrictions, if any, do you think should be made on gang-related music, movies, and use of the Internet? Explain your answer.

Chapter 6: Gangs and Society

1. What are some things your community could do to help prevent young people from joining gangs?
2. How realistic is the commonly held idea that gang members have lifelong loyalty to their gang?
3. The author says many communities are reluctant to admit that they have a gang problem. Why do you think this is?

ORGANIZATIONS TO CONTACT

Gang Reduction Through Intervention, Prevention, and Education (GRIPE)
East Coast Gang Investigators Association
90 W. Afton Ave., Suite #181
Yardley, PA 19067
E-mail: ecgiamanagers@gmail.com
Web site: www.gripe4rkids.org

With the belief that suppression tactics alone will not win the war on gangs, the GRIPE program concentrates on education and prevention and advocates teaching kids how and why they should avoid joining gangs.

Gang Resistance Education and Training (G.R.E.A.T.)
Institute for Intergovernmental Research
PO Box 12729
Tallahassee, FL 32317-2729
Phone: (800) 726-7070
Fax: (850) 386-5356
E-mail: information@great-online.org
Web site: www.great-online.org

Through the G.R.E.A.T. Program, police officers visit classrooms to educate students about gang prevention and to provide life skills kids can use to avoid gangs and make positive choices for their future.

National Gang Intelligence Center
Crystal City, VA
Phone: (703) 414-8600
Fax: (703) 414-8554
Web site: www.justice.gov/criminal/ngic/

The National Gang Intelligence Center tracks the growth, migration, criminal activity, and associations of U.S. gangs and provides this information to federal, state, and local law enforcement agencies and the public.

National Youth Gang Center
Institute for Intergovernmental Research
PO Box 12729
Tallahassee, FL 32317
Phone: (850) 385-0600
Fax: (850) 386-5356
E-mail: information@nationalgangcenter.gov
Web site: www.nationalgangcenter.gov

Funded by the U.S. Department of Justice, this organization provides information, resources, and tools to the public to help reduce gang activity using suppression, intervention, and prevention tactics.

National Youth Violence Prevention Resource Center
PO Box 10809
Rockville, MD 20849
Phone: (866) 723-3968
Fax: (301) 562-1001
Web site: www.safeyouth.org

This organization provides fact sheets, press releases, articles, and other resources to teens, parents, and teachers seeking information on youth violence in their schools and communities. Its goal is to help communities identify, address, and prevent youth violence in the form of gang activity, bullying, school violence, and more.

Books

Christopher Forest, *Gangs and Gangsters: Stories of Public Enemies*. Beaverton, OR: Velocity Business Publishing, 2010. With chapters that focus on some of the most notorious and deadly gang figures in the United States in the past century and ending with a discussion of modern street gangs, this book gives an interesting overview of gang history in the United States.

Lauri S. Friedman, *Dangerous Dues: What You Need to Know About Gangs*. Bloomington, MN: Capstone Press, 2009. This book examines what life is like from a gang member's point of view, from getting into a gang and living the gang life to getting out and moving on. It includes stories from people who have been involved in gangs.

Clive Gifford, *Gangs*. London: Evans Brothers, 2006. Full of quotes from gang members and photographs of gang life, this book offers different viewpoints on some of the most common questions and controversies about gangs.

Hal Marcovitz, *Gangs*. Edina, MN: Abdo, 2010. This book discusses the evolution of gangs through U.S. history and the modern uprising of gangs throughout the country, from cities to rural towns.

Stanley Williams, *Life in Prison*. San Francisco: Chronicle Books, 2001. Stanley "Tookie" Williams, founder of the Los Angeles Crips gang, wrote this book while he was on death row in a California prison. He describes his gang existence and how it turned out. As part of Williams's crusade to deter young people from gang life, his book shows the ugly realities of gangs from an insider's point of view.

Internet Sources

Ted Chamberlain, "Gangs of New York: Fact vs. Fiction," *National Geographic News*, March 24, 2003. http://news.national geographic.com/news/2003/03/0320_030320_oscars_gangs .html.

Sam Dealey, "America's Most Vicious Gang," *Reader's Digest*, January 2006. www.rd.com/your-america-inspiring-people-and-stories/americas-most-vicious-gang/article19854.html.

Hilary Hylton, "The Gangs of New Orleans," *Time*, May 14, 2006.www.time.com/time/magazine/article/0,9171,119401 6-7,00.html.

Kevin Johnson, "Drug Cartels Unite Rival Gangs to Work for Common Bad," *USA Today*, March 15, 2010. www.usatoday .com/news/nation/2010-03-15-rival-gangs-drug-wars_N.htm.

Web Sites

Gangland USA (www.newsweek.com/id/54180). The interactive "Map the Gangs" tab at this page on the *Newsweek* Web site allows users to click on any state on the map to find out what gangs are prevalent there or to click on a particular gang name and see which states it operates in.

Robert Walker's Gangs or Us (www.gangsorus.com). With content written by a gang consultant and former police officer of fifty years, this Web site provides descriptions of various gangs, ways to identify the presence of gangs and gang members in a community, video clips about gang life from gang members and leaders, resources for gang prevention, and more.

DVD

American Gangs, DVD, written and produced by Greg DeHart, A&E Home Video, 2000. This DVD traces the origins of gangs throughout U.S. history, showing how gangs have lived and operated over the years, how society has affected them, and how they have affected society.

INDEX

PICTURE CREDITS

Cover: ©Trevor Snapp/Corbis
© Ace Stock Limited/Alamy, 35
AP Images, 21, 50, 52, 58, 63, 70, 76, 80, 84, 85, 88, 94
After William Bengough/Bridgeman Art Library/Getty Images, 15
© Bettmann/Corbis, 18, 25
© Jonathan Blair/Corbis, 16
© Andrew Butterton/Alamy, 43
Jose Cabezas/AFP/Getty Images, 32
© Geoffrey Clements/Corbis, 9
Matthew Craig/The Commercial Appeal/Landov, 46
Ron Galella/Wire Image/ Getty Image, 72
Erik Hill/MCT/Landov, 65
Zhang Jun/Xinhua/Landov, 56
Robert Nickelsberg/Getty Images, 29 39
Paramount/The Kobal Collection/The Picture Desk, Inc., 69
David Pierini/MCT/Landov, 40
Reuters/Landov, 61
Jacob Riis/Archive Farms/Hulton Archive/Getty Images, 13

ABOUT THE AUTHOR

Jenny MacKay is the author of nine nonfiction books for middle schoolers and teens. She has a master of fine arts degree in creative writing from National University and lives with her family in northern Nevada, where she was born and raised.